CLOUD
MIGRATION
HANDBOOK VOL. 1

A Practical Guide to Successful
Cloud Adoption and Migration

José Antonio Hernández
Ammar Hasayen • Javier Aguado

ISBN: 978-1-6847-0921-2 (sc)
ISBN: 978-1-6847-0923-6 (hc)
ISBN: 978-1-6847-0922-9 (e)

Library of Congress Control Number: 2019912862

Lulu Publishing Services rev. date: 10/16/2019

To my nephew Sergio and the memory of Katy, an angel of love

Contents

Foreword

I think there will be a world market for maybe five computers …
Thomas J. Watson, IBM president, 1943

Currently in 2019, I predict that that there will be a world market for maybe five Clouds. Technology is a current global tsunami that is changing the world insofar as businesses, people, human relationships, education, politics, security, health care, and organizations, among others. The entire world is changing faster than it ever has in the past, thanks to the technology that encompasses the mobile Internet, digital cities with digital citizens; Internet of things (IoT); advanced robotics; autonomous vehicles; digital health, education, and experience; analytics; digital virtual and augmented reality; blockchain; machine learning; robotic process automation; natural language processing; natural nets; and artificial intelligence (AI). The common denominator of these new transformational technologies is Cloud computing, which provides the hyperscalability, flexibility, and computing power necessary to permit them to grow, expand, and ultimately change the world.

Cloud computing, which began only a few years ago, has also revolutionized human and business relationships throughout the world because it helps all businesses in many different areas, such as pay-per-use IT resources, IT cost reduction or flexibility, data security and management, IT collaboration, system integration, IT scalability, IT accessibility, DevOps, automation, and, of course, regulatory compliance (e.g., the General Data Protection Regulation [GDPR]).

When we think about technologies actually running businesses, many new Cloud computing trends come to mind, which will have a great impact on costs, flexibility, agility, scalability, and accessibility.

For example, service meshes aim to connect, discover, monitor, and authenticate communications between containerized microservices. Similarly, we find great utility in serverless computing with interconnected containers; managed containers (e.g., kubernetes); managed security; Cloud consolidation; open-source software (e.g., GitHub); Hybrid Clouds (e.g., Azure Stack); AI; and edge computing. At the present time, the trend receiving the most hype is quantum computing, a new computing power never before envisioned that will perhaps make my prediction of *five Clouds* a reality in the near future.

For all these reasons, I believe that *Cloud Migration Handbook* written by José Antonio Hernández, the current founder and chief technology officer (CTO) of myCloudDoor, is of great help for discovering how to start adopting or migrating your company's IT resources to Cloud computing.

A native of Huelva, Spain, José Antonio, a well-established writer of seven books (detailing essential skills for SAP technical consultants, e.g., *SAP R/3 Handbook* or *SAP Implementation Guide*), speaks from the point of view of experience, arising from his service as CTO for a variety of global consulting companies and helping small and very large customers in their Cloud migration projects since 2011.

This book is the key to unlocking the door to the future, one that will revolve around Cloud computing.

Marcos de Pedro, CEO, myCloudDoor Consulting Inc.

Preface

(By main author José A. Hernández)

It was not easy to write any of my previous books—all of them about SAP technology—and it has not been effortless to hold on to my belief in the brilliant future of Cloud computing when I started to evangelize about Cloud around year 2010, and mostly getting objections, concerns and excuses, which were probably the right thing to get at those initial times of the Cloud hype.

Despite being a firm believer in how important, useful, and beneficial Cloud computing would be for innovation and technology within organizations, at times I thought about just letting it go. However, around 2015, I started to get the attention of some people and companies that were early adopters of Cloud models and strategies. I did not give up because of them, and I really want to thank them for helping make my ideas a reality. They gave me the opportunity to put in practice what I had in mind and what was already available from Cloud vendors, and they gave me opportunities to fail, succeed, and learn more every day.

In the early days of the twenty-first century, around 2001, my company and I were closely involved with Microsoft in setting up and migrating SAP customers to the Microsoft platforms (Windows NT, Oracle, and the initial releases of Microsoft SQL Server), which created a really good working relationship and even friendship. Then around the end of 2014, I was told about the imminent release of SAP solutions on the Microsoft Azure Cloud, which got my attention.

Soon after, my colleagues and I started to make our first Cloud tests and migrations and saw the potential of the Cloud. At the beginning of 2016, I was exposed to real and complex Cloud migration projects, and the idea about writing a book to detail the process of adopting and migrating to the Cloud started to take form. But the pace with which Cloud services and technologies evolves is so fast that I knew by the time I could publish the first edition, it would probably contain obsolete material. This is still true, even if the first edition of this book is being released in 2019.

It is because of the enthusiasm of my colleagues at myCloudDoor, the expertise of my amazing friends, and the fact that I have always believed in teamwork and sharing knowledge and experience that this book is now a reality.

Acknowledgments

First and foremost, I want to thank my colleagues and friends who helped me out greatly in writing the first volume of this book: my co-authors and friends, Ammar Hasayen and Javier Aguado. Thanks to Javier Tabernero, Juan Carlos Ruiz, Daniel Guerrero, and Alex Saada, who have also helped with material and examples in this book and the second volume.

I also want to thank my friend and partner, Marcos de Pedro, president and chief executive officer (CEO) of myCloudDoor, for his confidence and help through these past years, as well as other colleagues and friends at myCloudDoor who have shown support and collaboration to make this book a reality: Fernando López, José Ramón Sierra, Marta Cantón, Jorge Flores, and Pepe Felipe.

Very important for me has been the confidence and trust of the many companies, organizations, and Cloud visionaries. There are too many people to mention, but I would like to highlight the confidence and enthusiasm of Luis Ramos, chief information officer (CIO) of Adveo group; Hans Koolen; Henk van Roosum; and the Philips Cloud Migration team.

I want to give special thanks to my friends at Microsoft who trusted and helped my company and me into the world of SAP on Azure, especially Markus Kruse, the person who encouraged my interest in the Public Cloud.

Finally I want to thank Alon Goldin and Issy Ben-Shaul from Velostrata (currently part of Google Cloud Platform), who showed me amazing technologies for overcoming Cloud migration challenges.

Introduction

Picture this scenario: the CEO or president of your company calls you to her or his office and tells you that she or he thinks the company needs to be much better at providing solutions for customers and users alike and much quicker at coming up with innovative ideas and products. She or he thinks that part of the problem is that your company's current IT model is too slow and not efficient and agile enough. She or he has been told that adopting and transitioning to Cloud computing could improve business and operations. So this is the request that she or he does to you, whether you're a CIO, IT director, VP of technology, or a trusted employee:

> *I want you to come up with a plan and a budget to transition our systems and applications to a Cloud computing model. I want it with minimum risk not to disrupt our current ongoing business operations, and of course it has to be highly secure and compliant with the must-have regulations of our industry and the countries where we do business.*

Of course you want to do such a great job and impress your CEO (or president) that you tell yourself, "I have to be perfect."

That's probably one of the most frustrating imperatives that anyone can tell us—or even to ourselves—and you might even find that if you strive for perfection from the first moment, it might be a big stopper for activity and usually a big-time cork for creativity.

Expectation of one being always perfect is a great responsibility and a large stressor. Think about those musicians or writers who, after coming out with a great album or book, had the pressure of making another perfect best-selling work. Many artists could not pass this test and instead drifted away in history and creativity, often because they were not able to reach other people's expectations of perfection … and also because "perfection" is a moving target.

On the other side—and not really in contradiction with perfection—there is the pragmatism. Summarizing briefly from Wikipedia, *pragmatism* was a philosophical trend in the late nineteenth century, based on the idea that the function of thought is as an instrument or tool for prediction, action, and problem-solving. Pragmatists contend that most philosophical topics—such as the nature of knowledge, language, concepts, meaning, belief, and science—are all best viewed in terms of their practical uses and successes rather than in facets of representative accuracy. And it's worth reviewing the synonyms: *practical, functional, utilitarian, realistic,* and so on.

We believe that we can get more value when starting projects or works with a pragmatic approach that at least will get us moving, acting, and doing, and then we can strive to incrementally improve it, like on a road to perfection, like from good to great.

In a transition or adoption to Cloud computing, we support the idea of starting with clear business goals (but not too many) and from there take a pragmatic approach that leads to a step-by-step design and deployment but without losing sight of the big picture, the business, its customers, and the users' requirements.

The value of being pragmatic is one of the core values of Cloud computing. For example, do you really need to specify in a request for proposal (RFP)/request for quotation (RFQ) all the complexity involved in the computing elements (operating system, memory, database, etc.) to implement the ultimate configuration of the order-to-cash process when the business goal is to gain market share for the wonderfully designed shoes you sell? Or would a modern Cloud customer relationship management (CRM) software as a service (SaaS) solution with out-of-the-box integration with your enterprise resource planning (ERP) suffice?

Just to name a few, here are some of the benefits of taking a pragmatic approach when transitioning to Cloud:

- You can define a secure and practical architecture based on business processes and goals and not on technology for technology's sake.

- You can have faster, quicker proof of concepts and/or working prototypes and start improving incrementally from there (e.g., one of the principles of the design thinking frameworks for innovation).
- You can save big on implementation costs. If you take the most standard and critical processes implemented first and define your set of must-have configured processes since they are the 80 percent of your business, then polish them in incremental improvements. That also implies a decreased risk of failures.
- With the Cloud, even the small companies can have a good plan for disaster recovery and business continuity.

When transitioning to the Cloud, recall this advice:

- Go for a practical approach on security. Odds are, your Cloud providers have much bigger, costlier, and many more security certifications than your company will ever need.
- Don't go for a big bang. Not only is it risky, but you might find the company and its ecosystem unprepared for too many changes.
- When deciding for SaaS, go for as much configuration (standard) and as little customizing (nonstandard) in your Cloud software. Remember Pareto's principle—80 percent standard processes and 20 percent customized ones. However, the cost of doing them is proportionally inverse. That 20 percent of customization will take 80 percent of the costs and the resources.
- Discovering and Analyzing your current systems and applications environment is critical for any other step along the way of adopting or migrating to Cloud. It will become the basic pillar for design, migrating and servicing your virtual data center in the Cloud.

When transitioning to Cloud, you don't need to be perfect. Just try to be a perfectionist, step by step. Way to go for innovation.

What This Book Is About and How to Read It

This book covers one of many practical approaches for adopting and migrating on premises, systems, and applications to the Public Cloud. Needless to say, the Cloud is not a one-size-fits-all suit. There is no unique approach, solution, or methodology.

We believe that this book stays at an intermediate level of technicality. While some chapters and sections start from basic concepts that anyone, even a person without previous knowledge, can read and understand, other sections and chapters require a firm technical foundation.

In order to fully understand this book, you will need a good level of IT data center general knowledge and expertise and a familiarity with basic Cloud concepts and terms. Some of these concepts are introduced and explained in the second chapter. To comprehend the technical examples included in different sections of this book, you will need a firm level and experience with virtualization, security, and scripting languages.

This is actually the first of two volumes that make up the *Cloud Migration Handbook*. While this first volume covers the foundations for adopting and migrating to the Cloud, the second volume deals with the design, deployment, migration, and optimization of your Cloud workloads, services, and resources.

Although we try to be Public Cloud vendor–agnostic, the reality of our team is that we have been more exposed to projects and experience using Microsoft Azure; therefore you can expect that most of the examples covered in both volumes are based on Microsoft Azure Cloud.

The following is an excerpt of what you will find in the six chapters of this first volume:

- Chapter 1 introduces the enterprise journey to the Cloud and the stages that organizations typically take when adopting Cloud up to the optimization phases. Then we explain our Cloud migration master plan, a general roadmap that should encompass most of the needs, requirements, and situations that you will find in any Cloud migration project. You will also find what to expect and what to do before you start a migration to the Cloud, the technical and organizational challenges you will most likely find, and finally, a checklist to assess how well prepared your company or organization is for the Cloud journey. There are topics that are of critical importance for a Cloud migration or simply an initial adoption, and they will be more specifically covered in each of the subsequent chapters, always trying to provide a practical approach and avoiding excessive discussions of scholarly debates or definitions.
- Chapter 2 introduces the Cloud basics as a way of exposing Cloud foundations and terminology to all stakeholders in any Cloud adoption or migration project. This serves as the Cloud acknowledgment phase within the master plan. It defines the characteristics, delivery models, and types of Cloud, providing practical examples. Then as a way to better visualize the Cloud, we expose a table with some of the most common differences between the most common and traditional on-premises systems and its Cloud counterpart. You can also find those important factors when deciding between types of Clouds and delivery models and what currently the reasons for moving to the Cloud are, the reasons for not moving to the Cloud, and the risks of not doing so. Readers with a basic understanding of IT can read and comprehend this chapter.
- Chapter 3 introduces the types of migrations to the Cloud and what to do when you are confronted with every type of system that needs to be analyzed for feasibility, whether they can or cannot be migrated to the Cloud and how. Types of migrations include replacing, rehosting, replatforming, upgrading to Cloud-enabled platforms, or refactoring. Then we go into some of the technical options you might find to

perform actual migrations and how to move your data into the Cloud. Then we introduce what types of systems and applications are not suited to move to the Cloud for technical or other reasons (e.g., compliance). We finish the chapter describing some scenarios for Cloud adoption, which can differ a lot in many organizations. To comprehend this chapter, some intermediate IT technical level and knowledge is recommended.

- Chapter 4 introduces what Cloud governance is and what its components are in order to establish the rules and processes for the efficient use of the Cloud resources that will be supporting the business applications, operations, and strategies. Topics explained in this chapter include organizational and human aspects of the Cloud governance model, demand and cost management, and those issues that must be considered closely when negotiating contracts with Cloud providers. We cover other aspects of the Cloud governance that are especially important for the adoption and migration to the Cloud (e.g., Cloud Reference Architecture [CRA]). Security management in the Cloud or the Cloud service management have their own full chapters in both volumes. IT Professionals at any level can read this chapter.

- Chapter 5 explains in detail the Cloud Reference Architecture (CRA), a set of documents that defines the roles, activities, and functions of the Cloud and its relationships. The International Organization for Standardization (ISO) standard that defines a CRA includes four different views, but what we explain in detail is specifically the deployment view. This view provides the rules by which Cloud resources have to be designed, set up, and deployed in order to maintain a standard within organizations, by which every Cloud service or element being used is correctly set up. This chapter includes real and practical examples of a CRA deployment view based on Microsoft Azure, that is, how to organize the enterprise structure and its Cloud subscription, the naming conventions for the different Cloud elements, and the resources to be technically deployed. We go deep into detail about identity and access management as well as the networking, security, monitoring, and business continuity management.

- Chapter 6 is about security management in the Cloud as a critical part within the Cloud governance model and its function to protect your enterprise's information assets. It explains how to set the stage for security in the Cloud, which requires a review of the shared responsibility model introduced in chapter 2. It then presents how Cloud security differs from traditional on-premises security management. You will also find here extensive sections about data protection in the Cloud, along with information about what is available and how to be better prepared and protected. It also goes into detail about identity and access management, compliance, and security threads in the Cloud. We finalize the chapter by introducing other additional topics related to security that are taking prominence within the Cloud, such as machine learning or the just-enough administration (JEA), and what is changing in security. Again, all the practical examples included in this chapter are based on Microsoft Azure.

The second volume of this book includes those topics within the master plan that are considered already part of the Cloud migration projects or belong to the optimization phase of the Cloud journey. This is a very brief extract of what you can find in the second volume:

- Chapter 1 (7) is discovery and workload analysis, which includes the tasks of assessing and making an inventory of your current infrastructure, platforms, and applications in order to perform a deep analysis on the feasibility of the migration, integration aspects, dependencies, design requirements, or testing needs. This chapter outlines the information required to be able to design and deploy the systems in the Cloud for the migration and prepare to run migration testing.
- Chapter 2 (8) deals with Cloud designs and deployments. Getting the input from the previous workload analysis and based on a CRA, your Cloud architects need to perform both high-level and low-level designs for the right architectures that will be deployed in your Cloud subscription that better meet your technical and business requirements. We introduce the topic of designing Cloud

architectures and the methods of deploying Cloud services with practical examples.

- Chapter 3 (9) deals with the methodology and activities recommended for performing migrations to the Cloud, taking into consideration previous preparations, technical challenges, and solutions that you might encounter, along with those aspects of Cloud governance that must be prepared for live operations (e.g., security and service management).

- Chapter 4 (10) introduces service management within Cloud governance, that is, how to manage and support your data center in the Cloud, from incident and security management to monitoring, alerting, and configuration management. Service management must be prepared and tested before you have systems and applications operational in the Cloud. No matter whether these systems are development or production systems, they need to be monitored and supported in the Cloud.

- Chapter 5 (11) deals with how to enter into the maturity or innovation phase within the enterprise journey to the Cloud and aspects of the migration master plan such as cost and workload optimization. It goes very deeply into automation capabilities that the Cloud can offer.

- Chapter 6 (12) contains a set of tools and template documents that you can easily adopt for your adoption or migration projects. It has explanations of each of the accelerators that you can use, such as analysis documents, design templates, runbooks, project plans, CRAs, checklists, and more.

1   The Cloud Migration Master Plan

Information and references coming from the market, vendors, competitors, and the media has reached one or more decision-making stakeholders at your company. Digital transformation and mainstream availability of Cloud services have surpassed hype point. The enterprise and company management are increasingly convinced of the benefits of Cloud computing and the need to start the Cloud journey, but they don't know how to start, how much it will cost, what the tangible benefits will be, how to do it right, and so forth. Those questions, needs, and requirements are normally forwarded to the CIO, CTO, or IT director for answers (and for the budget).

By 2019, your company might have already started adopting or migrating to the Cloud. If not, be sure that it will eventually have to take that journey—unless IT obsolescence and lack of agility affect the capacity to compete or innovate.

In this book are many sections where we will introduce reasons and benefits for going to the Cloud along with this journey's risks and challenges. In this chapter, we will introduce what experience has shown us to be the logical steps when a decision to go to the Cloud has been taken.

We have named these steps the *Cloud Migration Master Plan*. This chapter introduces this master plan with an overview of each of the stages and activities within it, which will be detailed in subsequent chapters of this book (volume 1) and the second volume.

It's not easy, cheap, quick, or minus its multiple challenges, but the journey will be worth it. And in many cases, it can be critical to business survival in a globalized and competitive market. But before getting into details, let's look at the most common way that enterprises start their journey to the Cloud.

1.1   Enterprise Journey to the Cloud

Many, if not most, enterprises have already started the journey to the Cloud, an evolution of how they provide, use, and innovate from the more traditional IT processes and resources to the new ways that the Cloud can do in a faster, scalable, more agile, and, when done correctly, more economical way. (It is either less cost or less total cost of ownership [TCO] for the same resources and services at the same service level agreements [SLAs].)

This evolution to the Cloud is often referred to as the enterprise's journey to the Cloud, as shown in figure 1.1. Each company does this journey at its own pace, but it shows a common way of starting the trek.

We typically divide this journey into four phases. As your enterprise moves to the following phases, additional gains and benefits can be obtained. These are typically measured in agility from a business perspective and savings from an economic one.

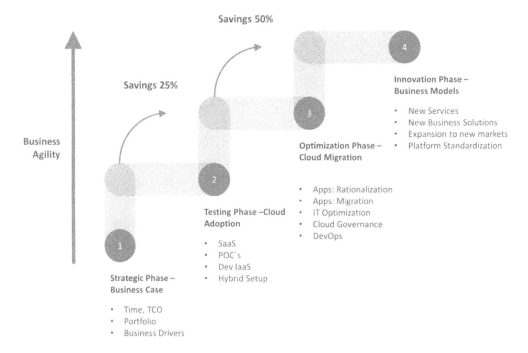

Figure 1.1 – Enterprise Journey to the Cloud

Let's look into the Cloud journey with some additional detail. The four main phases that you will commonly see are the following:

- **Strategic Phase: Making the Business Case**

  At the initial or strategic phase, companies start evaluating the possible implications of adopting Cloud computing. From a practical perspective, companies need to understand what the Cloud is and how it differs from traditional IT. They also need to comprehend the potential benefits, risks, security, compliance and data control, and impact on the organization and IT. At this stage, most enterprises start getting some training, IT and Cloud assessments, first internal analyses, and depiction of roadmaps, often with the help of consulting companies. Among aspects being considered at this stage are timing, ways of contracting cloud services, costs, TCO, portfolio of systems, and apps that could be the first candidates for Cloud adoption. And most importantly, they look at business drivers. They ask, "Can Cloud computing help increase efficiencies and strategic objectives for the company? Are business and IT as usual enough to maintain and increase market position? Is the digital transformation in our business really required in an economic and institutional world that is increasingly engaging and transacting through mobility with increased intelligence?" If your answer is yes, then be assured that Cloud computing and Cloud services are behind all those new capacities.

- **Testing Phase: Start of Cloud Adoption**

  At this stage, the easiest way for companies to start adoption and testing is to use Software as a Service (SaaS) solutions, which are usually not business-time critical like CRM, human resources, accounting, collaboration tools, or office productivity, such as Office365 and G-Suite. When considering other aspects, such as in-house development or thoughts about moving business-critical solutions (e.g., ERPs, warehousing, and production), it's the time companies start contracting and deploying Infrastructure as a Service (IaaS) and Platform as a Service (PaaS) and doing first pilots and proofs of concept. At this stage, when starting IaaS for noncritical applications, such as test or development environments, it's also the time for designing the first hybrid setups. In practical terms, it is providing networking and communications between end users and the resources deployed in Cloud and connecting sites and the on-premises centers, which everybody calls the Private Cloud. At this stage, it's important that at least basic Cloud governance is defined in terms of deployment, security, and compliance. Whether these tasks are going to be performed in-house or with the help of external Cloud professionals, it's useful for IT to start receiving technical training to better understand capabilities as well as risks. You don't want to get your company exposed to any external or internal threats. Public Clouds are well prepared to be safe and secure, and they provide lots of services and options, but this does not mean you don't have to design and deploy your security policies. In chapter 5, we discuss in detail the most important aspects of Cloud security for either adopting or migrating to the Cloud.

- **Optimization Phase: Cloud Migration**
Once the organization is convinced of the benefits that the Cloud model can provide, this phase is the natural step or actual door to a more mature Cloud strategy to obtain the impact and benefits being pursued. The most common topics that are decided and started during this phase are the following:

  - **Decision on a Cloud-first strategy**. Briefly defined, this strategy means that for every new IT service/application/system that the business requires, the first option will be a Cloud-based solution that adapts better to the users' and business needs.
  - **Cloud migrations**. As a logical consequence of the Cloud-first strategy, this phase is when migrations to the Public Cloud are decided and performed, the main topic covered in this book and its second volume. You will see in the next section that there are many aspects that need to be prepared technically and organizationally to guarantee successful Cloud adoptions and/or migrations.
  - **IT Cloud governance**. Another important aspect that is usually covered during this phase of the Cloud journey has to do with

setting up an IT Cloud governance as the way of organizing and optimizing the IT resources that are provided to the business.

- **Establishment of a Cloud-first strategy**. Migrating to the Cloud and establishing a Cloud-first strategy is going to directly bring a rationalization of the IT in terms of operations, management, security, support, and a more powerful and flexible DevOps environment.

- **General optimization of workload and costs**. Migrating to a Cloud IT model can bring significant savings to the organization, but a word of caution: to achieve those much-promised benefits, governing the Cloud, designing optimal architectures, bringing the power of automation, and managing the costs are of essential importance. All these topics are covered in detail and with practical examples throughout this book and the second volume.

- **Innovation Phase: Business Models**
Before Cloud computing, all sorts of innovations, in the form of new products or services or improved efficiencies, were constantly taking place in all types of private and public organizations and institutions. And the exponential advances in technology and computing, in particular, were key enablers for that. The Cloud is a step forward, an evolution proving unprecedented capacities for innovation, and it probably is a more democratic way since it allows even smaller organizations to take advantage of computing power and resources that previously could be only purchased with deep pockets for investments. The innovation phase is when companies start realizing the potential and most benefits of the Cloud: the agility to innovate. It's not just costs that can be saved. It's mostly the time that is needed to develop and put in place new services and products to reach a greater market and to more efficiently serve customers and citizens alike. Time efficiency translates into savings, including taking much less time to procure IT resources in a more optimized and automated way. The Cloud is an improved gateway to a world of possibilities to design and develop new business models in a globalized marketplace.

1.2   All-Cloud and Cloud-First Strategies

Nowadays for start-ups, most, if not all, of the IT resources and applications they need and use are 100 percent Cloud-based, an all-Cloud strategy. And as introduced in the previous section, for those companies and enterprises that have been operating for many years and with legacy (pre-Cloud) IT environments, a Cloud-first strategy is being introduced and adopted in many of them.

There are many ways for companies and public institutions to approach a Cloud-first strategy, due to many reasons from compliance to specific local markets as well as products and services. A practical view of what a Cloud-first strategy means, in simple terms, is that when there is a need for a new system or application, when it is possible and the business requirements are met, a SaaS solution will be adopted. If it is not available or specific business processes and requirements are not being met, a PaaS solution is chosen to build upon(*). And last but not least, if neither is an option, an IaaS approach will be taken.

When thinking about the Cloud market, IaaS is still the most consumed type of delivery model because the first approach when migrating to Cloud is to somehow replicate the way that IT has been provided, organized, and managed within organizations. It's also due to the fact that most of the applications being used were developed either locally on infrastructure (servers, storage, and network) or acquired commercially from software vendors that were designed (even with many different types of architectures) for traditional on-premises types of systems.

A Cloud-first strategy also means every existing system and application within the company will be moved/migrated to the Cloud when possible. If neither possible nor economically feasible, it will be put on hold for potential decommissioning when the right time comes and a replacement is found and available as a type of Cloud service.

In summary, any new application or project that needs to be implemented will be Cloud-based, and all current systems and applications will be either migrated to the Cloud or substituted by a Cloud-enabled system, application, or other type of Cloud service.

Depending on the current state, quantity, and complexity of systems and applications within the company, a Cloud-first strategy is usually planned as a multi-year type of program (from two to five years) in order to create the least possible disruption on ongoing business.

Looking at some numbers and predictions by IT analysts and distinguishing among start-ups, midsize businesses, and large enterprises, most agree that start-ups are almost 100 percent already full-Cloud based. The same thing will happen with small business when they do have a "full Cloud service but mostly SaaS approach." By the middle of next decade, over 60 percent of both midsize and large enterprises will be full Cloud.

1.3   The Cloud Migration Master Plan

The Cloud migration master plan is built as a baseline framework from which most Cloud migration (or adoption) projects can be represented. In some cases and certain specific typology, it depends on the degree of maturity in the Cloud of the enterprise undergoing a migration.

From a practical point of view, as we have based this book on real projects, we believe you will find all the necessary steps and activities under the different sections of this book and the following volume.

1.4   Cloud Migration Defined in Practice

For the purpose of this book and as it was already introduced in the preface, we are considering Cloud migration only when moving systems and apps from traditional on-premises to the Public Cloud. There are many different types of possible migrations. We discuss the approach for this in detail in chapter 3.

It is now very common to identify on-premises data centers with Private Clouds, commonly considered the same thing. We believe these traditional on-premises data centers are not Cloud, considering the characteristics defined by National Institute of Standards and Technology (NIST), but we will accept that common IT language, most often marketing misled by traditional hosting, collocation, or outsourcing companies and even for many hardware and software vendors.

There are, of course, other types of what could be called Cloud migrations, which we are not considering as part of our approach and are already happening … and possibly will see more often in the near future:

- **Migrating from on-premises apps to a SaaS application**. We consider this type of migration adopting a new SaaS-based app with an implementation project associated that most likely requires data migration, local customization, and integration.

- **Migrating among SaaS solutions**. This is a similar approach to the previous type, with the difference that your information is not stored on your premises but on your SaaS vendor. We already see that SaaS vendors are providing tools and resources to make this migration process easier to customers.

- **Migrating from two different Public Cloud providers**. -Quick evolution of capabilities, pricing and contracting makes enterprises to decide for a multi-cloud strategy approach to avoid potential vendor locked-in. We are seeing more often the migration from one public Cloud vendor to a different one.

The order of the master plan below can be slightly changed depending on the degree of your current knowledge, exposure, and experience to the Cloud, and of course, it's by no means the same "implementing a software as a service application" than migrating your current IT environment to the Cloud.

We came to develop this migration master plan after dealing with several different types of migrations we got exposed to and with the inestimable help of our colleague consultants, customers, and even other partners involved in the project.

As a way to organize and make the migration master plan (see figure 1.2) easily understandable, it is composed of three stages: premigration or preparation stage, migration stage, and optimization stage.

• Cloud Migration Master Plan

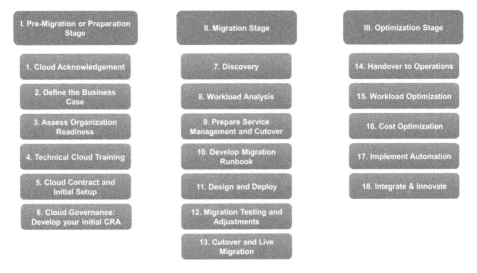

Figure 1.2 – Cloud Migration Master Pllan

Let's have a closer look at each stage and the steps within each. Please note that both volumes of this book are actually about explaining each of those steps in detail and from a practical perspective, so this is just an introduction. Each step will reference which section, or even a full chapter of this book deals with that step in-depth.

1.4.1   Cloud Pre-migration or Preparation Stage

This is what the organization and the team need to know and what should be prepared before starting any type of a Cloud migration project. This spells out the best understanding on the Cloud and Cloud migration. The better the organization is prepared and aware at every level, the less surprising and smoother the process will be, possibly at fewer time and cost. The preparation stage includes:

- Cloud acknowledgement and enablement
- Definition of the business case for the Cloud
- Cloud readiness assessment
- Cloud technical enablement

- Initial Cloud contracts or subscription setup
- Plans for a new or updated IT/Cloud governance and development of a CRA
- Dealing with security and compliance

The recommended master plan steps within the pre-migration stage include:

1. *Get trained and acquainted on Cloud computing.* It is essential to become familiar with Cloud computing terms and definitions, types of delivery services, and what they have to offer. And it's very important to have a crystal-clear concept of what Cloud computing really is and is not, and there is no better practical way than to see the differences between traditional IT on-premises services and the ones that Cloud makes available. You cannot even think about adopting or migrating to the Cloud if you don't know where you are going and, most basically, if it is even technically feasible. This book introduces a practical overview of Cloud basics, which you need to know before any migration project.

2. *Develop a business case for the Cloud.* Companies need to find and justify the reasons why the business needs to transition to the Cloud model, all from an economic, technical, and mostly strategic perspective. Therefore a business case is necessary. A business case is more than calculating just the TCO. For instance, how do you measure the time required for demand and capacity planning? How do you measure the differences in the capacity to innovate (whether we are talking about new or evolved products and services, a fresh way to relate with your customers or partners or provide improved efficiency to your production processes, etc.)?

3. *Acknowledge enterprise readiness for Cloud.* One of the most common issues arising when adopting and moving to the Cloud is to suddenly discover that there are certain aspects and processes within the organization that will have to be changed and were not taken into consideration. This might provoke inefficiencies, delays, and potential disruption in the business itself. A process of change management is highly recommended: assess and analyze how ready your organization is for those changes that are coming and what will and have to be changed in

the organization and its processes for moving to the Cloud. Examples of potential changes that enterprises need to prepare are: demand management, financial models, compliance, support, contracting, and others. And from a technical perspective, examples are networking, latency, performance, business continuity planning, SLAs, and others. This topic is analyzed in more detail later. You can also find a template example of how to check and review your company readiness for the Cloud and how to assess the Cloud maturity level subsequently.

4. *Get your IT staff technically trained on Public Cloud concepts.* The role of IT departments, whether you are normally doing your own admin or only project management, is likely to change when moving to the Cloud. Therefore it becomes absolutely necessary to train your IT staff on the Cloud and do it in an organized way so everybody within the company and your providers talk identical languages and understand the same way of governing the new way of delivering IT services to the business. Having your own internal Cloud architect(s) will provide huge benefits, not only because you will be able to target your needs in a more accurate way but also because you will be able to control and manage the costs in a better and more economical fashion. It's quite common and a good practice to look for external help in architecting and managing your Cloud services, but don't let the business depend on that. IT's role will change, but not as drastically as many papers and blogs have been announcing. At the end of the day, the purpose of IT was—and still is—in the Cloud to provide technical solutions to the business and to adequately maintain those solutions. The recommendation at this stage is to attend Cloud training, whether online or on-site, or contact expert consultants to train your staff. Perform Cloud assessments, which depending on the depth can be very useful for the discovery phase within the migration stage. But since Cloud assessments should involve a deep cooperation, involvement, and information exchange between IT and consultants, they are very helpful to realize and comprehend in practicing Cloud concepts. Of course, if your company is doing proof of concepts (e.g., deployment of a managed instance group, migration of a database, deployment or migration of a SAP system, security baseline Cloud setups and testing, etc.), make sure that your IT and other stakeholders

are actively involved. A few days or weeks of testing in real time is probably one of the most efficient ways to become proficient in Cloud concepts. We have included what we believe to be a comprehensive overview of the most common Cloud concepts and services, as usual with a practical focus. We compare how to work and manage Cloud services differently from traditional on-premises services.

5. *Develop Cloud governance and a CRA.* Consider Cloud governance as the operating model evolving from traditional IT governance but now with the characteristics and power offered by Cloud computing. The way of organizing your data center(s) in the Cloud requires an operating model, a precise and structured method to define the policies, procedures, and processes that must be implemented within the company to guarantee the optimal use of the Cloud resources from portfolio management, SLAs, service management, and costs. IT Cloud governance is a very extensive topic, which we deal with in detail in chapter 4. A very important topic that relates heavily into Cloud adoption and migration—before it should be performed—is the CRA, which defines the roles, activities, and functions of the Cloud and its relationships. It provides a methodological framework for the deployments of all Cloud projects, based on the defined architecture, security standards, and regulations. The ISO / IEC 17789 is an international standard for the definition of a CRA (http:// standards.iso.org/ittf/PubliclyAvailableStandards/index.html). The ISO standard identifies four views, as shown in the table below:

USER VIEW	Context, parts, roles, and activities in the Cloud
FUNCTIONAL VIEW	Necessary functions to support Cloud computing activities
IMPLEMENTATION VIEW	Functions necessary for the implementation of a Cloud service, with what types of elements or services
DEPLOYMENT VIEW	How Cloud functions are technically implemented within the Cloud infrastructure elements

Table 1.1 – Cloud Reference Architecture Views

From a practical and technical perspective for Cloud adoption or migrations, the deployment view is the more important CRA view. It's important to consider that usually the CRA is a live "document" in terms that new Cloud services can be adopted, where you might want to define how to deploy them in your company or subscription. Chapter 5 talks in detail specifically about the deployment view.

1.4.2 Cloud Migration Stage

This is the phase where testing and live migrations take place, but to perform successful migrations, the systems and apps to be migrated must be discovered and analyzed; target systems architecture and security have to be correctly designed, deployed, and configured; and service management must be ready from the very beginning.

Additionally you must consider all feasible and technical migration options to meet your goals and requirements. This stage, specifically for migration projects to the Cloud, requires the use of some type of methodology or methodological framework. We are introducing one that we have successfully used often, which we named "Agile Cloud Transition Framework." Activities within this stage include:

- Complete discovery and workload analysis
- Prepare service management (an important part of the Cloud governance)
- Develop your migration protocol(s) (runbook[s])
- Design architecture and deploy your target systems
- Perform test migrations and adjustments
- Execute live migrations

Let's introduce these activities within the master plan:

6. *Complete assessment and discovery.* Discovery is the process of making a detailed inventory of systems platforms, applications, integration, networking, and all types of requirements (business, technical, costs, etc.). Of crucial importance for successful migrations is early identification of aspects and issues that might cause errors and lead to too many post-migration adjustments and problems. Examples are

hard-coded IPs, scripting, and third-party programs. Findings and discovery documents will be used as the input for the subsequent phase of analyzing the workloads to be migrated. A great deal of the discovery can nowadays be partially automated using discovery and assessment tools, which are available in the market, but the company will have to provide other required information. We cover this topic in detail and with practical examples in chapter 7 of the second volume of this book.

7. *Complete workload analysis.* Throughout our experiences leading and performing migration projects, we came to realize that this is the stage that most enterprises overlook more (fortunately not all). We consider this phase the most important of all (besides proper planning). The best and more detailed analysis is performed, the easiest, quicker, and less risk will show up during the migration. The objectives of workload analysis of the systems/apps to migrate are to:

- Establish if migration to Cloud is feasible and what the technical options are (direct, tooling, etc.)
- Analyze dependencies (integration, service management, security, contracts, user access interfaces, networking, communications, etc.)
- Establish migration priorities and grouping (if required)
- Build the test plan and specific migration protocol (runbook)
- Prepare the test/live migration and fine-tune the process and runbook
- Define the full migration planning
- Get requirements for the design
- Obtain requirements for the admin, support, and operations (monitor, alert, backup/restore, batch, printing, transport, third-party products, etc.)
- Anticipate needs for networking and firewalling rules for integration and interfaces

Results from this activity will be the output in the form of an analysis document containing deliverables such as those in the table below:

Migration Feasibility
Migration Technical Options
Requirements for Admin and Operations
Architecture and Security Design Requirements
Networking Rules
Dependencies
Migration Protocol / Specific Runbook / Test Plans
Optimization and Scripting Requirements

Table 1.2 – Workload Analysis Expected Output

Of course, each migration project is different, and the extent and scope of how and what your business needs for a Cloud migration might be customized to your business' specific requirements. Chapter 7 of the second volume of this book explains in detail and with practical examples how to perform the workload analysis and which type of output you can expect.

8. *Prepare service management and cutover planning.* Although introduced in the pre-migration stage, Cloud governance involves many IT and business processes. This stage only takes into consideration those aspects related how to service the organization and its underlying technology (in the Cloud), so this is the stage or moment to prepare how you are going to provide services to your new data center in the Cloud, handle a smooth transition, and monitor the apps. This stage also sets up how support will be provided and systems need to be operated and managed. The cutover is the process of transitioning in an orderly way from the source systems and on-premises applications to the new Cloud-based services. That will include careful planning to make the process as least disruptive as possible. When done right, most of the time, end users basically do

not notice any difference in their daily work. It can be, however, a bit different for those people in charge of security and administration of the systems and communications. At this stage, a plan for this transition should be developed and communicated properly. We deal with service management and cutover in detail in chapter 10 of the second volume of this book

9. *Develop your migration protocol (runbook).* As with any type of project, a detailed planning of all steps, which will be required to perform a successful migration, is an absolute requirement, where step-by-step activities are clearly established with responsibilities and timing. In the case of a Cloud migration, this is known as the migration protocol, or commonly referred to as *runbook*. If this is the first time, you can develop it as an iterative process since for sure it will not include all activities from the very beginning. If using external expert help, they should come with previous similar runbooks and/or templates that can be a starting point. The migration protocol is also a frequently updated resource, which usually gets additional steps when performing test migrations before actual live migrations. And while some of the activities can be the same or very similar in all types of migrations, often it will be required within specific areas of the runbook according to the systems and applications being migrated. So if you are migrating a full data center, you might need several protocols according to the specifics of each application being moved. They can be quite comprehensive or include only the critical aspects of the migration itself. This is up to project management, but with the experience, we came to realize that including all activities from the migration phase we have described in the master plan is a good practice. You can find examples of the sections, including how to design migration runbooks, in the second volume of this book in chapter 9, as well as in the migration tool kit. (Refer to chapter 12 of second volume.)

10. *Complete Cloud architecture design and deployment.* Before you can actually migrate, most likely you have to perform a high-level design of your landing zone in the Cloud and then convert that to a low-level design by assigning values to the different Cloud service elements and components that will be deployed and configured. If your company

has followed a logical process of the pre-migration steps, you should at least have some type of deployment view of the CRA that defines the rules of your virtual Cloud data centers and greatly facilitates the assignment of values and provisioning of all the security and authorization measures, as well as the structure and organization of all Cloud elements and services that will need to be deployed for your migration. Even in the case of using migration tools that does the deployment for you of some Cloud elements (subnets, virtual machines [VMs], storage, etc.), you will have to perform a design and maybe adjust the deployment values of these elements that migration software deployed.

11. *Perform migration tests and make adjustments.* For every important migration, it is very convenient and oftentimes absolutely mandatory to perform a migration test run and, sometimes, if there are several issues, more than one. Migration testing serves many purposes:

- Check if the runbook is correct and make any amendments (if required)
- Benchmark the actual migration, which is extremely important in migrations of critical apps, which require minimum or near-zero downtime, to the Cloud
- Perform thorough testing (as previously planned and defined during the analysis phase) on the migrated system: application testing, technical testing, integration testing, and so forth
  - For any tests that do not pass, there might be the need to perform some corrections or adjustments that must be carefully documented and included within the runbook. Pay particular attention to integration testing: those that test connectivity with satellite systems—whether inbound or outbound—since this is the one aspect of the migration project that usually triggers more errors due to firewalling, changed IPs, or DNS settings. Or occasionally for inbound connectivity, the adjustments are performed in the satellite/connected system and not in the migrated one.
- Test compliance requirements
- Test security requirements and policies

Take into consideration the time it takes for performing all the testing and validations since in the real live migration, you might not have that amount of time. Extremely careful planning and very well-documented adjustments are a must. Also if there are adjustments that could be applied before the migration without having any live impact, it should be also realized as soon as possible.

12. *Execute cutover and live migration.* Cutover is the process of stopping any activity or operation in the source system and starting to work in the migrated system, so again, this is a process that must be planned and carefully designed within the organization and documented in the runbook. Otherwise chaos might happen at live migration due to typical problems such as application users unable to connect (IP addresses, not resolving DNS, firewalls, etc.) Live migration will be the actual migration. A rollback and point of no return should be considered in case any critical issue is found that could potentially affect the business. Once the migrated system is live, it must be serviced and supported from the very beginning, so make sure that all the service management is ready and has also been tested. That includes monitoring, operations (backup/restore), second- and third-level support, ticketing, and so on. We explain a thorough cutover and live migration in detail in chapter 9 of the second volume.

1.4.3 Cloud Optimization Stage

Even if you have performed a successful migration, to truly benefit from all the Cloud has to offer organizations, at this stage you should pay attention at all the optimization possibilities that the Public Cloud offers, which will help enterprises to benefit from savings and increase performance. They can also increase efficiency through automation. Activities within this stage are:

• Hand over migrated systems to operations
• Workload optimization
• Cost optimization
• Automation
• Integration and innovation

13. *Hand over to operations and support.* Service and admin support for your Cloud subscription, your Cloud services (whether infrastructure, platform, and any other type of Cloud services you use), and the technical support must have been ready and prepared, as we have introduced in the section about Cloud governance and the procedures tested as part of the testing phases and activities. At this stage, whether it's going to be performed internally or externally, the support and operations must be taken care of from the very moment that a workload or application is going to be used productively. (That not only means production environment. A development or testing environment must be just as important.) The way to hand over a migrated or newly deployed system normally requires a structure procedure where all stakeholders are informed, prepared, trained, and ready to provide the support and operation services they will be requested. It's important that in order to hand over systems to work productively in Cloud, all compliance and security requirements should be ready as well.

14. *Execute workload optimization.* Workload and cost optimization can be considered as the two faces of the same coin since they are very much related. Optimizing workloads has more to do with finding the most optimal design and Cloud architecture (while there is no single answer for a perfect design). Could the same results be achieved using different Cloud services? PaaS instead of IaaS? Do we really need high availability? Can the data be archived? Can we reduce the size or service type to better match real needs, using auto-scaling on scale set or managed instances and other procedures for optimizing, such as taking advantages of automation capabilities in the Cloud for service snoozing (stopping and starting the systems at predefined scheduled) for ad-hoc starting and stopping and many others? Refer to the chapter and sections on Cloud design as well as in chapter 11 of the second volume regarding automation capabilities in the Cloud.

15. *Review cost optimization.* Although closely linked with workload optimization, which can also have an impact on costs, optimizing saving costs is more focused on
    • which and how the services were contracted,

- if you can use lower or less costly services based on the measured average use,
- which type of cloud services (pay per use, reserved instances, burst instances, other ways Public Cloud vendors offer customers for further discounts, etc.),
- auditing for unused services (hard disks, reserved IPs, etc.),
- possibility of bringing some of your previous on-premises licenses for applications, databases, or operating systems, or
- if your software maintenance contracts can be also migrated to the Cloud release or matching service.

16. *Implement automation.* At this stage, of course, in one way or another, you should have already started developing automation for many previous topics within the master plan. For instance, although it's usually quite straightforward to deploy a Cloud service using the vendor-provided portals, normally for professionals, this is better achieved by writing or using previously developed scripts that will perform automatic deployments or automating the installation of target systems for a newly adopted Cloud service or the target platform of a migration. Automation is not new or only relevant for Cloud computing, but the fact is that a Public Cloud offers a view of an infinite pool or resources is much easier and it provides more possibilities for automation than traditional on-premises systems. For example, you can automate VM deployments without worrying too much if there will be availability, but options are endless. Here are just a few examples:
    - automate start and stop of systems and apps at scheduled times or at request
    - automatically deploy all type of Cloud services using scripting languages or automation tools
    - automate the testing of your developments
    - provide automated DevOps CI/CD without the need to stop your apps for upgrading

    In chapter 11 of the second volume of this book, you can find detailed explanations as well as the many ways and examples of how automation can make a difference in your move to the Cloud, along with the method to gain unprecedented efficiencies .

17. *Integrate and innovate.* Getting to this stage is where enterprises really start to profit and benefit from the advantages that Cloud computing brings in. Here, the potential examples are endless, and the best way to really appreciate is when comparing how your company would do it in traditional IT. Because most new apps and systems are being released to be directly run on the Cloud (whether SaaS or PaaS mainly), they come with many possibilities for allowing tight integration between Cloud services, like those provided by serverless (Cloud functions), message queues in the Cloud, and close integration of productivity tools (Microsoft Office, Google Docs, etc.) with native Cloud services. Mobile, Cloud analytics, big data, and the IoT are just a few examples of the endless possibilities for taking full advantage of the many ready-to-consume services the Public Cloud can provide to enterprises. In chapter 11 of the second volume, we discuss and introduce with much more detail why and how to integrate and innovate, all thanks to Cloud. Just imagine this couple of examples:

- A service management tool within your company (for ticketing, service requests, or IT needs) allows a business user to request a new development system or any other type of Cloud service (normally previously defined in the catalog of available services) with a simple form, including the required information (reason, timing, cost center, type of app, approver, etc.). And once approved, the request triggers a template or script (infrastructure as code) that automatically deploys and installs the required service (even with the required timing: start times, stop times, period, etc.) and informs the user that her or his requested service is already available. And this is all done in a few minutes or a handful of hours.

- Your company is expanding its business to other international geographies where they need to run an ERP system or a Business Intelligence system but with their local flavor and requirements (taxes, legal, security, compliance, etc.). With Cloud, you can prepare an image of the baseline ERP to be specifically configured and localized and make it available in the required (or closest) region where the apps will be used for the business. The hyperscalability of the Cloud is almost a safe bet in the sense that you will not have problems with lack of resources when automating deployments. (Of course there are checks to be done, like enough quota in the subscription or cost limits that the Cloud subscription owners might have defined.)

1.5   Before You Start a Cloud Migration Project

As introduced in our migration master plan, we strongly recommend a good preparation (the objective of what we have tried to cover in this book) to be prepared for change and disruption on the way to delivering IT services and applications to the business and, of course, careful planning and testing. Yes, there might be some type of disruption in several business processes within organizations, but notice that the same disruptions can bring great benefits and competitive advantages to enterprises and institutions.

Before you embark on a Cloud adoption or migration, get prepared and don't overlook:

- Cloud economics: variable costs, budget, security, and compliance issues
- Staff and stakeholders' preparation
- Cloud governance as an evolution of your IT governance, with special care to define and develop an initial CRA

Make sure to take care of the compliance and security policies and requirements. Prepare for the right design to cover your requirements, both technically and legally. Engage in careful planning, both in terms of project plan and migration protocol(s) (runbooks). Your project might be a simple migration or adoption of single or low numbers of systems and applications, or it might be a very complex, full on-premises data center migration to the Cloud.

It's key to understand that to get the benefits, cost savings, and efficiencies that the Cloud can provide, your company must find a way to tightly integrate the new Cloud computing model into its actual business strategy.

1.6   Challenges for Migrating to Cloud

The enterprise journey to the Cloud, as introduced in the first section of this chapter, can bring a myriad of benefits to your enterprise, but the road to the Cloud is not without many challenges, most of which are not foreseen initially, some of which are unexpected, and others of which are overlooked.

In general, you'll have to prepare and train or reskill your IT staff, change some business processes regarding IT financials, modify your IT governance to resemble the needs required by Cloud service and support procedures, redesign and rearchitect your security policies, guarantee your compliance regulations, and plan carefully whether you are going to adopt Cloud services for new systems and applications or your migrations. All of those challenges can be solved if there is a strong sponsorship and commitment from decision-makers and upper management.

As with all disruption and change within companies, Cloud adoption is a process that requires considerable effort from the entire enterprise. There will be natural resistance. Some types of resistance will have reasons, but many will probably be excuses and objections to any new or changed processes. This is the usual reaction to any changes, both in personal and professional environments.

The move of systems, application, and data to the Cloud will impact many enterprise business processes in the organization, and that's why strong commitment from the management is a must. More than ever, technology and business agility are key aspects for enterprise growth and survival in a strong and global competitive business landscape.

Management has to establish reasonable goals for adopting the Cloud computing paradigm. A migration to the Cloud requires a team effort to plan, design, and execute all the activities to move the application workloads and systems to the new IT based on consumption of Cloud services.

We are introducing the most typical challenges of Cloud adoption and migration in the following sections, organized in both technical and organizational challenges.

1.7   Technical Migration Challenges

From a technical perspective, a Cloud migration project can be quite simple or can be quite complex, depending on factors such as the migration scope as well as maturity and life cycle of workloads being moved. The way to find out is to execute a very good process of discovery and workload analysis.

If you find in your discovery and analysis phases that technical challenges are low complexity, then the migration should be much easier and faster. However, as the level of complexity and the migration challenges are higher and bigger, you should expect increased time and effort required for successful migrations. Let's discuss each of the complexity and challenges that you are likely to find.

1.7.1   Dealing with Integration

First and foremost, the most common complex issue you may encounter when performing a migration project is the level and complexity of the integration of the data, systems, and processes to be migrated. In medium to large enterprises, you don't usually find isolated systems, but interconnected applications, which can be tightly coupled at the business process or data level or can be used for reporting purposes. Dealing with integration in a Cloud migration project includes topics such as:

- application interfaces of different nature and types: online, offline, batch, synchronous, asynchronous, use of files, utilization of sockets, use of message queues, FTP servers, and so on
- data imports, exports, extractions, and conversions for loading reporting and analytics systems
- systems connected for running different type of workflows or BPM-driven processes

Typically you can also find integration not only between your internal systems and applications, but with different type of business partners you might be dealing with: customers, vendors, banks, third-party logistics, and others.

Integration challenges also have to do with the way that complex and multitiered systems are designed, architected, and set up: load balancers, web servers, application servers, database servers, presentation servers, and so on.

And probably the one aspect that has more impact on the smoothness of a Cloud migration is to be prepared that systems and application connectivity is set up correctly regarding security, access, and authorization policies, for example, issues such as firewall rules, ungranted permissions, network security groups, service accounts, domain controllers, and correct access to the proper resources that have to talk to each other.

In Cloud migrations, one of the most important aspects to deal with these issues is to perform a thorough discovery and workload analysis where you can identify and inventory all these integration needs, intersystems dependencies, and security policies.

So what can you do to be prepared and avoid trouble as much as possible when dealing with integration challenges? Here are some ideas, which we cover in detail in several sections and chapters throughout this book and the second volume:

- There are automated assessment and discovery tools that are able to find IP addresses, ports, and protocols used for incoming and outgoing connections. Watch out that this type of tooling cannot automatically discover all integration and dependencies.
- If you don't have or can't use automated discovery tools, try to create your own type of connectivity and integration inventory. Make sure to include integration and dependencies within the workload analysis. When possible, perform technical checks within the systems with administrator privileges to review any and all settings for configuring connectivity among systems.
- Often connectivity is set up inside the applications, so you will need the help and support of application owners, service managers, admins, or support personnel to stop them and be ready for the changes that it might have on impact in a migration.
- As much as possible, you should set up all your connections and firewall rules that require IP addresses using a DNS type of addressing

since a simple change of the DNS value could automatically resolve many of the problems when changing IP addresses in a migration. This should be a best practice when designing and developing any type of interfaces and integration in your company.

- Identify all the stakeholders involved in interfacing and integration that can be required and called upon in a migration to Cloud project.
- Mock integration testing is an absolute must in complex environments. That must be carefully prepared. It's also good planning for the step-by-step adjusting and correct configuration of interfaces and security controls. The recommendation is to be as specific as possible in your migration protocol (runbook) in regard to those activities. Refer to chapter 9 in the second volume of this book on practical examples.
- Regarding multitiered systems and applications, the key aspect in order to solve the complexity of moving these types of systems to the Cloud has to do with the designing and deployment of the target architecture. This can be a complex task since often there is no simple option for a redesign in the Cloud, and there might be many factors and considerations according to specific business needs. We deal with the topic of design and deployment in the Cloud in chapter 8.

Remember that integration is not an isolated technical issue when approaching a migration to the Cloud, but one that is tightly coupled with the other technical challenges we are discussing below.

1.7.2   Data Gravity and Downtime for Migration

Data gravity is a technical term that refers to the weight of the data within the data centers and the power of attraction that it has regarding to bringing together (attracting as the earth gravity) additional systems and applications. Most often this data is also dynamic, which brings additional challenges in a migration. It takes more effort to connect and transfer the amount and nature of data from source data centers to the Cloud. Since there is more data gravity, the more volume of data that needs to be transferred in an organized way to defy that gravity.

Closely related to how to overcome data gravity effects for a Cloud migration (even for a migration where only data is transferred), there are collateral issues such as the connectivity and the bandwidth available between data centers and the Public Cloud, integration technical issues (see section above), the dynamic nature of the data you might need to transfer, and the downtime that can be acceptable for the less risky disruption of daily business operations.

Overcoming data gravity issues can be addressed from different angles and with various technologies, for example:

- From a technical perspective, migration tools can replicate the storage or data while maintaining consistency and uptime of source systems, providing short cutover times.
- Most Public Cloud vendors offer their own migration tools and services (even the possibility of sending offline hard disk storage) to deal with this issue.
- When dealing with dynamic data, in particular, with transactional and operational databases, most include their own replication techniques the same way they are set up for clustering and high availability (e.g., Oracle DataGuard, Microsoft SQL Server Always On, or SAP HANA System Replication, just to mention a few), which can allow you to have a system on-premises and send the replication to the Cloud system. Additionally—and especially to deal with minimum downtime—the database log shipping mechanism can be used.
- Finally the order and grouping of workloads to be moved to the Cloud is a topic to carefully plan. While for single or simple systems with no or low dependencies, this can be quite straightforward. Complication starts with high levels of integration complexity and dependencies. To deal with that, workload analysis must take into consideration how to make the right logical move groups, organizing those workloads into groups that make sense to move together.

1.7.3   Compliance and Security

For many types of enterprises and the industry they belong to, it might be required to have different levels of compliance validations and security standards that must be met, wherever the systems and applications are located, whether on-premises or in the Cloud.

Cloud is a new way of delivering computing resources, not a new technology. Cloud computing provides the scale and flexibility that attract businesses due to many benefits like reduced capital expenses and increased agility and resiliency. However, this could have a good and bad impact on security as well.

From one side, massive concentration of resources and shared infrastructure can be more attractive to attackers, especially with the publicly accessible Cloud management application management interface (APIs). From the other side, however, Cloud-based security defenses can be more robust, scalable, and cost-effective.

Since migrating to the Cloud includes a third party (the Cloud provider) that offers services on your behalf, a new shared responsibility model evolves when adopting a Cloud strategy. The Cloud provider handles security of the Cloud while you are responsible for security in the Cloud. This means you should carefully understand what you are responsible for securing instead of assuming the Cloud provider takes care of it.

The Cloud also affects the way organizations deliver and measure compliance. In fact, the same shared responsibility model that applies to security also pertains to compliance. Compliance is a shared responsibility in the Cloud. Just because you are putting your data in the Cloud does not mean the compliance responsibility shifts entirely to the Cloud provider.

Only by carefully understanding how the Cloud operates and what you are responsible for securing can you establish a security governance that can work for the Cloud. Chapter 6 is fully dedicated to dealing with security and compliance for adopting or migrating to Cloud.

1.7.4   Networking, Connectivity, and Latency

Needless to say, your enterprise users and admins will have to connect and access their applications and systems from their sites, and to perform any type of move, transfer, or migration, you will need to set up connectivity between source sites to Public Cloud or Clouds (for those companies adopting multi-Cloud strategies).

Your operator of choice can provide connectivity and communications.

You might reuse all or part of your current communications, or you might additionally look at more modern, advanced, and faster options such as software-defined networks (SDNs) and other tooling that are able to create almost "on the fly" a new type of safe and virtual network. Public Cloud vendors are increasingly looking into making the process of new networking easier and faster, with many options to choose from.

Topics that present a technical challenge regarding the overall communication needs have to do with availability of tools and communication operators in the areas where you run your business. While this is not an issue in many countries, there are still regions in the world where setting up communications with Public Cloud is not easily available and might present issues such as high latencies, which might be unacceptable for certain business processes to operate properly.

Latency is the time it takes for systems or nodes to reach another system or node. It can be the one-way or round-trip time, and it's usually measured in milliseconds. In practical and simple terms, it is the delay between two systems to reach each other.

1.7.5   Supported Platforms

The feasibility, type of migration (refer to chapter 3), and available technical options for performing a successful migration to a Public Cloud will also depend on whether the underlying system platform, mostly the operating system and its release version, is supported or not (can be deployed and the vendor will provide maintenance and support) in the Cloud. There are other restrictions regarding what is and is not currently supported in the Cloud, which we explain in more detail in chapter 3.

In practical terms, the leading Public Cloud vendors only support 64-bit-based Microsoft Windows systems and most types and flavors of Linux operating systems (CentOS, Ubuntu, RedHat, Suse, Debian, etc.) and only from certain newer releases.

You can only find restrictions about using certain software or database engines on top of the supported operating systems in the Cloud. At times, due to actual technical restrictions, even if technically feasible, it might be that the software vendor does not certify or offer maintenance or support to their software on certain or all Public Clouds.

In general, what is now being called *legacy platforms* (e.g., those of mainframe computers, IBM AS/400, HP/UX, and many other older systems) cannot be deployed in the Public Clouds.

1.7.6   Understanding the Technical Differences

The summary of this section is to approach Cloud adoption or migration. Understanding the technical differences, capabilities, design options, and restrictions are a key aspect in the overall process. With the examples we are including throughout this book, we are trying to give a broad overview of these differences, mostly from a practical—and not deep—academic perspective. You can find many of the technical differences and restrictions in chapter 3, dealing with the different types of scenarios you might find when approaching a migration and the options available for each.

This is why the migration master plan includes the need to get not only general acknowledgement of Cloud concepts but also technical training. There are plenty of online and on-site training courses and materials. All major Public Cloud vendors offer many certification tracks and programs.

1.8   Organizational Migration Challenges

When transitioning your IT to a Cloud or hybrid model and whether adopting, implementing, or migrating to Cloud, challenges go beyond just the technical ones, which, with the right experience and maybe with external help and budget, can be achieved and accomplished successfully. It might seem paradoxical, but your organization might have some more trouble when dealing with those challenges coming from the organizational changes and the impact they might have.

In the sections below, we discuss the most important ones that you most probably have to deal with. Of course, the nature of your organization, for example, if you are working for a private profit and customer-facing enterprise or for a public organization and institution, will have different angles and challenges.

1.8.1   New Governance Model for the Cloud

Cloud governance is the definition of an operating model for the optimal use of the Cloud services provided to the organization, that is, a set of policies and procedures for the correct provisioning and use of the IT resources provided by the Cloud capabilities.

There are many governance models for traditional IT, based on different frameworks and standards (e.g., ITIL, COBIT, etc.). The challenge for governing the Cloud is how to evolve and adapt—or define—their IT governance models to the new Cloud-specific services and capabilities. Issues include how to adapt the new governance model to meet required SLAs, monitoring, service management, demand management, security, compliance, or other required quality or validation processes in enterprises and organizations.

In chapter 4, we introduce a pragmatic overview of one of the many possible Cloud governance models, including the following main components: CRA, demand management, security and compliance for the Cloud, service management, cost management, and process automation.

Governing your IT in the Cloud is a very extensive topic and most probably the basic technological pillar that includes all the processes that are needed for supporting the business.

1.8.2   Managed Cloud Services

Since the very first moment you have the first systems with a productive use (even if these are development environments), the organization needs to have in place the service management model and governance so systems are protected, secured, monitored, optimized, and managed and quality, security, and SLAs are met as required.

As an integral part of the new Cloud governance model, the challenge is to transition from the current on-premises model to the new Cloud model. We deal with this topic as a new way or model to do outsourcing or go a step forward even to have Managed Cloud as a Service (MCaaS). Consider now the shared responsibility model (next chapter), where your Cloud provider will be responsible for providing services that previously were performed either internally by your IT department or your service and support partner. We dedicate a full chapter in the second volume of this book on how to organize and be prepared for the new service and support management in the Cloud, along with all the required activities that must be considered.

1.8.3   Lack of Internal Experience

Even if the Cloud is an evolution of the well-known virtualization technologies, there will be many changes and skills required for your IT staff to get acquainted with. For some time, IT departments and even incumbent system integrators have been quite fearful of losing their current jobs because of the Cloud. This is not really the case; although it is true that many activities and responsibilities now lay on the Cloud provider. That is already included in the pricing, which IT, an outsourcer, or managed services provider previously performed. All of those activities related with hardware and infrastructure—replacing storage, plugging network cables, doing firmware updates, and so many others—do not add any value to the business. With Cloud, it comes as standard, along with many others depending on the delivery model chosen.

In technical terms, IT needs to be prepared and mostly reskilled, which is not difficult at all for system admins and support personnel. Training, good material, workshops, and assessments are a good way to accomplish this. A bigger challenge is the organizational one since there might be important changes and differences in the roles and functions that IT personnel will be in charge of. We deal with this topic in the chapter on Cloud governance as well as the impact on people within organizations, in particular with IT departments.

1.8.4   Change Management

Businesses and technology are in a continuous change state. There is a famous sentence from a big company CEO stating that "change is the only variable that remains constant." As a generic process, change might have many objects and processes within companies, but managing the change refers only to the most critical focus point: people.

Fear to change is intrinsic to human nature, and this is actually fear to the unknown. We change for two main reasons: when finding ourselves in a limit situation or when there is a model we want or need to follow. In the second case, the unknown transforms into the known. All people behave in a very mimetic way, so therefore the second reason it's comparable to the process of learning: the explicit knowledge becomes tacit. There has been a transfer of useful information. This will be the key to effectively manage the changes: the learning process.

Change, as an implicit continuous process, is a result of the need for surviving or improving so business can react and respond better in a more efficient and competitive way to customers, shareholders, citizens, business partners, and employees. Looking at efficiency and agility to reaction is the main reason—and not so much the cost—why Cloud is becoming the new standard for consuming IT resources.

There are market trends, financial figures, and new products, technology, competitors, needs, and so on. Currently it is unquestionable that change is important for business growth, and the Cloud model should be seen and handled as real business and strategic projects as well as the real enabler and pillar of most, if not all, technology needs. And it must be clearly seen how important Cloud technology and services are for driving change.

Cloud computing, in fact, has enabled an essential milestone in the role of business strategy, such as the possibility for extremely quick provisioning and procurement of IT resources and services, which is key to be able to react to the constant changes in markets, products, organizations, and, in general, the structure and objectives of companies. Organization readiness for the Cloud will require management of the changes that come with it.

1.9   Assessing the Enterprise Readiness for the Cloud

Whatever your company goals when starting or following your journey to Cloud adoption or migration, all share the need for assessing whether all levels of the organization are ready for the Cloud, but not for any Cloud, the one that better fits their purposes. Every business is different.

Needs are different, IT can be different, and their goals and needs for a Cloud transition will be equally different.

Even if some of the topics of a Cloud readiness assessment do not apply to your organization or if there might be others of your own, a readiness assessment is a great way to have the big picture of the road ahead and be able to plan accordingly.

Transitioning to Cloud is not a goal in itself. At least it should not be a technological goal, not even a project name or program, but a business one. In this sense, it's not that much different than implementing traditional on-premises applications and systems. Both types—whether Cloud or on-premises—enable business processes, efficiency, automation, intelligence, cost savings, compliance, and so on. In summary, they allow the business to run, operate, transform, and compete.

On implementing and transitioning part or all of your IT to a collection of Cloud services, just like in traditional on-premises IT, one suit does not fit all. Transition is not going to be easy, and there are quite a few challenges ahead, as we just introduced in the previous sections. One way to prepare is to check how ready your organization is for what lies ahead.

Let's look at some of these readiness topics and how you can assess the status of your company or institution.

1.9.1 Organizational Readiness

This first and global issue is the one that responds to the big question: What does it mean from an organizational point of view to be ready for transitioning to the Cloud? That involves the following questions:

- What will change in the organization?
- How will Cloud IT services impact the organization?
- Are we ready to communicate the changes?
- What will happen with roles, responsibilities, and job descriptions?
- Will the changes align well with company strategy?
- How will it impact our financials and operations models?
- How will the control of our data and security change?
- Are we ready to be compliant with the regulations?
- How much will business processes change?

Once the stakeholders come up with the answers, the way to handle the organizational readiness is to develop an organizational change management plan and execute it during the transition project.

1.9.2   Workplace Readiness

For business users to support new technical and business initiatives, they must be prepared, but they must also be involved, informed, and trained. Whatever comes with the Cloud, it must include clear benefits for the users: applications must be easier to use and to learn, they must help them accomplish their tasks more efficiently, they must be more informed, and they must provide more job independence.

Business users will be ready when they all see the clear benefits for the company and them. Having a new great user experience, like what they find in their favorite online website and their mobile apps, will certainly help with adoption. In order to check their readiness, the following aspects must be assessed:

- Do users have a technically suitable workplace or device for accessing the new systems?
- Will they need specific training?
- Are the business users involved in the project?
- Are they being informed? Are changes being communicated?
- Will the business user be able to perform some testing in a similar working environment?
- Do the users know how and when to contact support?
- Will the new systems and applications be aligned with users' requests?
- Will they be allowed for anywhere, anytime, any device access?

With the answers from the above questions, vendor recommendations, and best practices, a plan must be designed to make sure business users and their workplace are ready for the transition.

1.9.3   Technical Readiness

What are the technical requirements that need to be prepared and in place so a transition to the Cloud is viable and feasible from a technical viewpoint? Of course you won't be able to answer specifics until you also have done a workload analysis, but these questions will be useful for both tasks:

- Will the Cloud be able to handle our IT workloads?
- Are we ready to transfer our current IT governance model to the Cloud model?
- Do we have enough network bandwidth?
- Is there connectivity backup?
- Are we ready for integration intra- and inter-Cloud?
- Are we ready for new security?
- Are we monitoring-, operations-, and support-ready?
- Will there be a contingency plan in place?

1.9.4   IT Readiness

One of the traditional barriers of the last few years for Cloud adoption was the fear of IT departments that Cloud would take away their tasks and jobs to the Cloud providers and they would feel inadequately prepared for the new tasks. IT needs to adapt to the Cloud like it has adapted to any other IT technology that has been continuously implemented in their companies.

IT has been always adapting, so evolving to the Cloud shouldn't be an excuse any longer except for those who feel inadequate to keep on learning. The IT department is critical in the Cloud age for many reasons, but two are critical: because they must handle integration and governance. Checking that IT must get ready involves questions such as:

- Do we have—and will we have—the right IT governance?
- How will the transition change the service catalog and associated policies?
- Does IT have the skills, knowledge, and experience? Have they been trained?
- What additional expertise will be needed?
- How will we handle integration issues inter- and intra-Cloud?
- Will there be the need for new system management?

- How will SLAs be handled in the new Cloud context?

1.9.5   Cloud Transition Project Readiness

Except for the fact that depending on the different Cloud delivery models and types there are tasks for which the Cloud vendor is completely responsible, the Cloud projects will not be much different than if you are about to start a traditional IT project (if there were a way to define what a traditional IT project means), but whether you have implemented your e-commerce, did a previous data center migration, or configured or developed your ERP, email systems, or customer service applications, all of those projects have in common a set of very important factors, often critical for the successful outcome. In Cloud transition, there is no difference, so get ready with stakeholder commitment, budget, right personnel, right service partner, right Cloud provider, and proven methodology.

1.9.6   Ecosystem Readiness

Finally, make sure that you take into consideration what might be the most important element in your whole organization: your customers and other critical business partners such as vendors, suppliers, distributors, and so on.

If a transition to the Cloud is going to impact or change the processes in dealing in any form with your business partners, make sure you are ready for them. So in this case, just assess any potential change in your engagement processes and act accordingly by either communicating the changes with anticipation and preparing your business partner ecosystem.

Checking the readiness of the organization at all levels, as introduced above, is not an isolated process within a Cloud transition program. It is intimately related to:

a) The goals and objectives according to the business strategy
b) The governance model to set in place the grouping of policies and procedures for the optimal consumption of Cloud resources
c) The requirements and workload analysis from the technical perspective

d) The definition and execution of the change management plan from the people and process perspective

If you can get those four pillars—business strategy, Cloud governance, technical requirements, and change management—clear and ready, we believe your Cloud transition project is deemed for success.

1.10   Making the Business Case for a Cloud Migration

Cloud computing represents a fundamental change in how companies use and provide their services. For many small and midsize businesses, it represents a choice to compete in a business environment with powerful competitors.

Since Cloud adoption and migration is a topic discussed and analyzed in every company, it is clear that despite objections, which are becoming less of real reasons, most stakeholders are convinced of the benefits that the Cloud can bring to enterprises and their business strategies. However, when confronted with starting the journey or the project, there will always be a main question on the table: With Cloud, will we spend more or less money than with our current systems? From our perspective, this should not be the main business driver or factor to weigh and assess a business case.

Of course, it is essential for organizations to maximize the benefits of migration to Cloud architecture by reducing costs and minimizing risks. But typically we found that there is an essential factor for making the business case, time, that is overlooked or not considered sufficiently important. How long does it take to respond to business needs and requirements before and after Cloud models? And that is of crucial importance because quicker times and automation capabilities means unprecedented agility and therefore much less costs. It should not be too complicated to take time into the cost equation, at least at a high level.

Let's see an example with a real scenario. In our organization, we have decided to implement a new SAP S/4HANA solution.

Traditional On-Premises Approach	Public Cloud Approach
Perform required sizing (hours/days)	Perform basic sizing (scale up or down with simple redeployment) (minutes)
Prepare a RFP and ask for proposals for hardware/hosting vendors (days/weeks)	Select your VM from the Cloud marketplace (minutes)
Resolve the RFP, negotiate the contract, and issue purchase order (days/weeks)	Select if you want pay-as-you-go model or reserved instances (minutes)
Receive hardware, install, and configure (days)	Automatically deploy and install software (hours)
Install base platform and SAP software (days)	Already done
Landscape: a prod system with 128 CPUs and 4 TB RAM, a quality system with 64 CPUs and 430 GB RAM), and a development system with 32 CPUs and 256GB RAM and 2 regular application servers	Same landscape with VMs on Cloud
Estimated cost: around 300K USD CAPEX investment Time: at least six to eight weeks	Estimated cost: Around 9K USD per month OPEX costs Time: between four and twenty-four hours

Table 1.3 – Difference between On-Prem and Cloud Approach

Next, let's look at common factors for a business case of migrating to the Cloud, analyzing the costs and benefits. The next table shows an example with some common factors.

COSTS	BENEFITS
Assessment and discovery costs	System and applications landscape inventoried with current state
Workload analysis	Systems and applications analyzed
Cloud migration project	Prepared for a fast and agile digital economy
Training	New skills for IT employees
Licensing	Same or bundled licensing
Setup Cloud governance	New processes and policies allowing further costs and workload optimization
Managed services and support	Many services now included within Cloud costs
New OPEX and remaining CAPEX	CAPEX reduction/OPEX optimization
Setup security and compliance	Cloud security and compliance standard features and certifications far more advanced
Downtime costs	Better SLAs at lower costs
	Opportunities for quicker market expansion
	Focus IT on business strategy
	Risks of technology obsolescence

Table 1.4 – Making the business case for Cloud

Making the business case based on the previous table means to evaluate those costs versus the benefits, but it is important to not stay at the short term. Look at the midterm future of the company needs and strategy:

- If your costs are higher than the expected benefits, then maybe the migration to the Cloud does not make sense.

- If your benefits are clearly higher than the costs, then a migration and a Cloud strategy makes sense.
- If the result is about even, then you should make a reassessment of your figures or directly decide to go to the Cloud. Just find the right trigger and time to do so.

Now let's also look at common elements for making a general TCO calculation.

On-Premises	
Direct Costs	Indirect Costs
Hardware: Servers, storage, networking	Up-front investments
Virtualization software	Administration and procurement costs
Support and maintenance	Software licensing and asset management
Licensing	Capacity planning and adjustments (over/under)
Security, routers, firewalls	Life cycle management
Operations management software (monitoring, alerting, backup, etc.)	Setup and installations
Facilities	Contract management
Power and cooling	Training
Communications	Compliance
SLAs	Disposal costs
Personnel	Facilities and physical security management
Business continuity (clustering, disaster recovery, data center redundancy)	

Table 1.5 – Factors for calculating TCO

While on Public Cloud, you will still have some of the costs you find in the previous table. You don't have to manage or pay for many of those, and you no longer need to worry about them. All major Public Cloud vendors offer tooling through their websites to help organizations make this calculation.

Although initial calculations might only show some savings, when your organization reaches a maturity stage (innovation phase) on the enterprise journey to the Cloud, this is when the real benefits and the lower TCO are clearly shown.

2 Practical Foundations for Cloud Computing

Whether your organization is either adopting or migrating—or both—to Cloud, you need to understand and acknowledge what is and is not Cloud. This chapter serves the purpose of the first step in the Cloud migration master plan as we have introduced in the previous chapter and why it is important when taking the enterprise journey to Cloud computing.

At this stage of massive use and adoption of Cloud computing, most of you already understand and might have lots of experience with the Cloud, so this chapter is mostly intended for those readers who might not yet be familiar with Cloud concepts and terminology or those who are going to start their first migration projects. We are taking a more pragmatic approach, trying to avoid computer engineering, academic, and scholastic discussions and providing visual and useful examples.

We will not discuss definitions or history of Cloud computing beyond the most respected ones (NIST) and give it a pragmatic prism. What are the uses of Cloud computing? Could those uses be performed before Cloud? How do Cloud services differ from the traditional computing services? Why does everyone think it has revolutionized the way computing resources are provisioned, deployed, consumed, secured, and paid for?

When dealing with a migration project, you need to understand and figure out if the migration is feasible, what type of migration you will be confronted with, and if your system, application, workload, or, in general, you can meet the technological needs that support your business and its processes are available in the Cloud.

You will also need to design for the Cloud and operate and support your systems and applications in the Cloud; therefore you need to have a good overview of what Cloud computing is. And from our viewpoint, a good way to explain it is to compare it with the most traditional IT on-premises computing (you will also find that there are not only differences but many similarities): how you do it in the Cloud versus the way it's typically done on-premises (on traditional IT).

We have also included the most common themes and issues when an organization has to decide on what Cloud service model or Cloud type to use for their needs.

2.1   Evolution to Cloud: Technology and Digital Transformation

Cloud computing, the "disruptive technology" that we know and are using massively today (often unaware of), is the outcome on one side of the constant need to increase IT efficiency to support new business requirements and strategies —digital transformation. From another perspective, it's the technological advancements and innovations over time since we have become familiar with computer technology: more powerful and cheaper hardware, hyperconvergent systems, more advanced and reliable virtualization systems, better and broader networking, and the capacity of software in general to define and operate almost anything.

In the sense of the capacity and endless possibilities that Cloud computing has enabled, it can be considered quite revolutionary, but as introduced, it is an evolution of the technology that has been developed over previous years of computing.

For the last few years, "digital transformation" has been the buzzword responsible for moving all the strategic areas on enterprises and organizations alike to drive innovation, and business changed as a result of the massive use of social media, mobility revolution, analytics and AI, big data, and IoT, just to mention the most important ones. In order to have a base for driving that digital transformation, there was the need for a different type of computing technology, one that is hyperscalable, instantly available, and easily consumable.

Digital transformation is shaking businesses and organizations with an unprecedented speed of change and creating an impact that is altering industries, ecosystems, and people's lives. Digital transformation has acted as a catalyst for the massive adoption and migration to Cloud computing.

As end user, for sure you have been using directly Cloud services for a while now: it is the technology that supports all those social networks and mobile apps, messaging and mail systems, e-commerce sites (online shopping), online gaming, collaboration tools and services, shared storage, and so many more.

Without Cloud technology, it still could be possible to have many of those services, but it would be quite costlier without the elasticity and flexibility to quickly adapt resources to users' actual needs. And it's much more difficult to maintain, and in general, there's less reliability for growth and performance. Most of the new services coming to our daily lives are doing so thanks to the services and capacities provided with Cloud technologies.

2.2   Defining Cloud Computing

It seems that the origin of the name "Cloud" comes from the early days of the internet: interconnected systems sharing information and requests came from one side and came out from the other side. The diagrams for that broad connectivity were represented as a Cloud, in order to abstract what was happening in the middle: a complex network in charge of processing, accessing, and distributing information. And from a practical perspective, it really did not matter to end users.

In this sense, the naming has been probably a good one since abstraction is a very good analogy of what Cloud does and means today for the majority of users: Cloud is enabling unprecedented use of resources and applications by billions of users who do not really care how all that technology is being set up. For these users and also the majority of IT professionals, the Cloud acts as an abstraction layer for having the impression of possessing unlimited IT resources.

2.2.1   National Institute of Standards and Technology (NIST) Definition of Cloud

As per the definition of cloud computing by National Institute of Standards and Technology (NIST), *Cloud computing is a model for enabling convenient, on-demand network access to a shared pool of configurable computing resources (networks, servers, storage, applications, and services) that can be rapidly provisioned and released with minimal management effort or service provider interaction.*

It demonstrates five essential characteristics, three services models, and four deployment models of Cloud. Figure 2.1 is the most common diagram of Cloud computing at a glance.

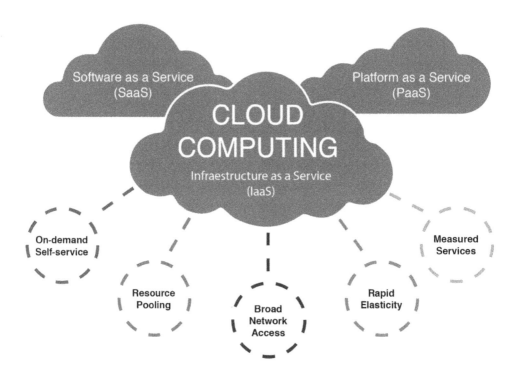

Figure 2.1 – Cloud Computing at a glance

2.2.2   The Five Characteristics of the Cloud

Let's look at the five characteristics that define Cloud computing according to the NIST.

1. **On-demand self-service.** This means provisioning or deprovisioning computing resources as needed in an automated fashion without human intervention. An analogy to this is electricity as a utility where a consumer can turn on or off a switch on-demand to use as much electricity as required.

In practical terms: A user can provision a Cloud service without asking for any human intervention in the Cloud data center, and this can be done through different mechanisms: the Cloud provider portal, via APIs, through a web or mobile app, or use of service management tools integrated with Cloud provisioning scripting languages or APIs. If you cannot do self-service to provision a Cloud service yourself without human intervention, then it's not really Cloud (with exceptions).[1] Let's start looking at some examples using two of the most widely known Public Cloud vendors: Microsoft Azure and Google Cloud Platform. Figure 2.2 shows an example of a screenshot of the Microsoft Azure Cloud when provisioning a VM.

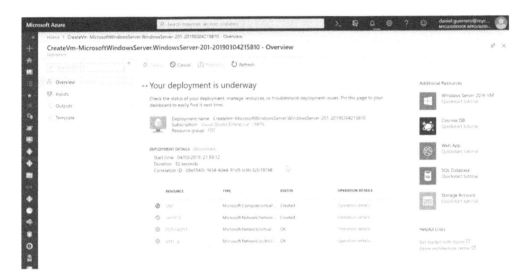

Figure 2.2 – Deploying a Virtual Machine on Azure

And below is an example of provisioning a VM using Microsoft Powershell scripting.

---

[1] This might be not the case in software as a service application, where there is the need for a subscription model that requires the Cloud vendor to provision the application in the Cloud for you.

Figure 2.3 – Deploying a VM on Azure using Powershell

Figure 2.4 shows a screenshot when provisioning a VM from Google Cloud Platform Console.

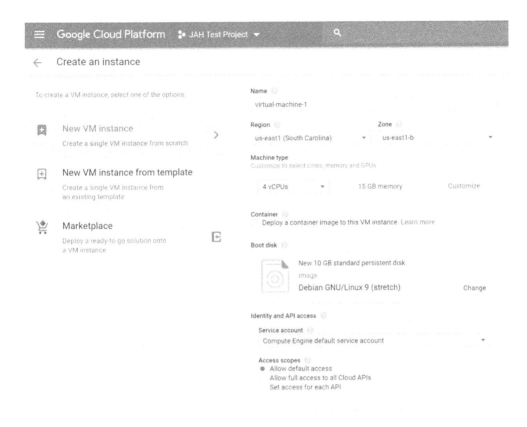

Figure 2.4 – Deploying a Virtual Machine from the GCP Portal

And in figure 2.5, it´s an example of provisioning a VM using Google Cloud Gcloud scripting.

Figure 2.5 – Deploying a VM using GCP gcloud utility

Figure 2.6 shows a screenshot for selecting an image for provisioning a VM from the Amazon Web Service Portal.

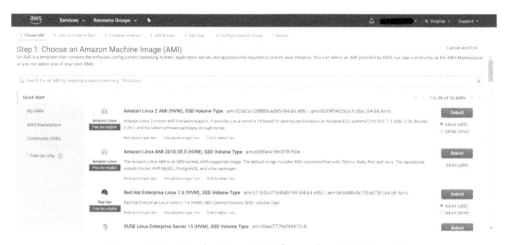

Figure 2.6 – Deploying a VM from the AWS Portal

And below it´s an example of provisioning a VM using AWS scripting.

Example AWS script to provision a VM

```
aws ec2 run-instances --image-id ami-abc12345 --count 1 --instance-type t
2.micro --key-name MyKeyPair --security-group-ids sg-1a2b3c4d --subnet-id
subnet-6e7f829e
```

Figure 2.7 – AWS command for provisioning a Virtual Machine

2. **Ubiquitous network access.** This means that computing facilities can be accessed anytime and from anywhere over the network using standard communication and access protocols and any sort of system or application clients.

   In practical terms: A Cloud resource provided as a service—such as a VM, an application, or a platform—can be accessed from TCP/IP using a remote connection (e.g., RDP or SSH) or application clients (e.g., a SAPGUI for SAP systems located in the Cloud) or just when using your apps from your smartphone, tablet, laptop, or any other device. For example, as long as you have network connectivity, you can access your electronic books or favorite music streaming service or even manage your company systems from your office in Houston, your apartment in Buenos Aires, or a nice beach in the south of Spain.

3. **Resource pooling.** This means that computing resources available in the Cloud (which in Public Clouds are available at a large scale) are pooled to meet the demand of the consumers so resources can be dynamically assigned, reassigned, or deallocated as per requirements. Generally the consumers of Cloud services and resources are unaware—remember "abstraction"—of the exact location of those computing resources, although, if you look at previous images, you are normally able to specify locations (regions, zones, and the like) where they want to provision those resources.

    In practical terms: Pooling the resources (e.g., storage, memory, processing, networking, software, etc.) is the way of obtaining economies of scale for Cloud providers, so a resource not being used or being released by a user can be available for others to provision and consume. Cloud resource pooling gives a sense of infinite and immediately available IT resources. For the purpose of visualizing this characteristic, an analogy of pooling is the software "multitenant" model.[2] The same physical resources are shared into pieces used by different users into distinct units. For example, if a host (physical server) in a Cloud computing center has the capacity to serve/create ten or more virtual servers, it most often happens that different consumers are using those virtual servers.

4. **Rapid elasticity.** Cloud computing provides an illusion of infinite computing resources to the users. In Cloud models, resources can be dynamically and elastically provisioned or released according to demand. In this way, it is much easier to scale up or down your resources to the real needs and use of the computing resources.

---

[2] Multitenancy is a type of computer architecture that usually applies mostly to software applications, where a single instance of that application is serving multiple customers or users.

In practical terms: Let's set up the example of a company online shop (e-commerce site). You might be a local shop or an international one, and it's often the case that your site has more traffic and orders at different time periods, such as when launching a promotion or on Black Friday. So at times you need less resources, and at peak demands, you need many more resources to handle the load and customer requests if you want to provide the same level of performance—remember that people don't wait too much on websites when they are unresponsive or too slow—and the same level of reliability. Another example for companies with business management systems (e.g., ERP) that needs to do finance consolidation once a month or run huge reporting periodically, it happens exactly the same: with traditional on-premises computing, you would need to have the IT resources to be able to handle the peaks, while with Cloud resources, they can be adjusted to actual needs and periods. When the peaks are no longer required, unnecessary resources can be automatically released. Actual example of these capacities and functionality available in popular Public Cloud providers are the Azure scale sets, the managed instances in Google Cloud Platform, or the AWS auto-scaling.

Measured service. This means basically "pay per use," like utilities. Cloud consumers only pay for the computing resources they use and when they use it, although when consuming SaaS, most often the way of measuring consumption and paying for it might be subscription and per user-based and variants of that model.

In practical terms: This concept of measured services is similar to consuming electricity, gas, or water. But Cloud provides many extra benefits to this concept. A good example is the capacity for "snoozing" resources, like automating start and stop of servers (VMs) that are not required to be up and running 24/7. This is being frequently implemented for systems used for development, training, testing, demo, and other purposes, which are only used at certain times, at certain schedules (e.g., automating start Mondays to Fridays from 8:00 a.m. to 6:00 p.m.), or ad-hoc (always down and started on demand). Organizations these days can rely on the Cloud service providers to get computing resources on-demand and in an automated way, along with paying only for the resources they have used and avoiding unnecessary expenses. From these Cloud characteristics, we start to see some key aspects of the benefits that Cloud is bringing to users, organizations, and businesses alike: hyperscalability, cost savings and economies of scale, pay per use, efficiency, and agility. These are just the baseline for the many advantages that these bring all together. You will find several sections in this chapter with specifics about the reason for moving to Cloud in any delivery model.

2.3 Cloud Delivery Models

Cloud delivery models refer to the way that Cloud services are delivered to users and organizations for consumption. The three main delivery models are:

- **Infrastructure as a service (IaaS).** It is the delivery of computing infrastructure as a service. That includes mainly servers (CPU and memory), storage, and networking. Examples of IaaS are Azure Virtual Machines, Google Cloud VM Instances, and Dropbox shared storage. More information and examples about IaaS are provided in a chapter section below.
- **Platform as a service (PaaS).** Providers deliver not only infrastructure but also middleware (databases, messaging engines, etc.) and solution stacks for application build, development, and deployment. Example of PaaS are provisioning Wordpress site, Google App Engine for developing mobile applications, and Azure SQL Database. These PaaS services are mostly provided from the Public Cloud vendor marketplaces. Figure 2-8 shows an example of provisioning an Azure Web App resource.

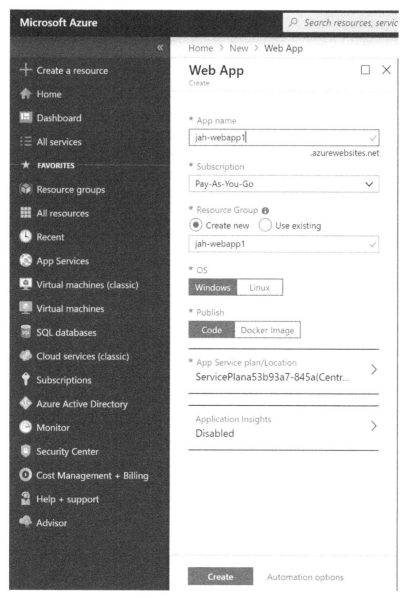

Figure 2.8 – Creating a Webapp from the Microsoft Azure Portal

- **Software as a service (SaaS).** Applications hosted by a provider on a Cloud infrastructure are accessed by thin or thick clients over the network or a program interface (e.g., web services). Examples are Google Docs, Office365, Saleforce.com, and Quickbooks Online.

The actual difference between these delivery models relies mostly on up to what level of the technology stack is the service provided by the Cloud vendor, which implies the share of responsibility of the Cloud vendor versus the share of responsibility of the consumer.

Figure 2.9 shows graphically the concept of sharing responsibility in the Cloud delivery models.

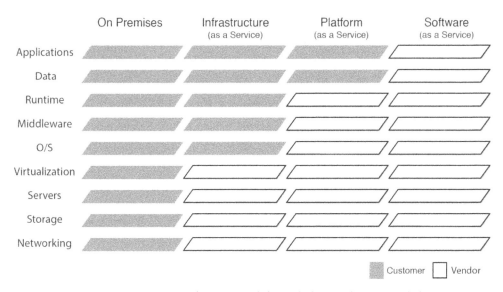

Figure 2.9 – Cloud Delivery Models and Share of Responsibility

There are, of course, other differences at the software engineering and architecture levels, such as the way that those services are provided and the APIs they use for being consumed properly, but for practical purposes, we will leave those technical details at the abstraction level.

There are other delivery models of Cloud services emanating from these main types of services, although they are just specialized variants of IaaS or PaaS mainly for specific needs, such as Disaster Recovery as a Service (DRaaS), Database as a Service (DBaaS), and Communications as a Service (CaaS).

It is also very common for both customers and managed service providers to play with the semantics of these delivery models. For example:

• Providing IaaS and Managed IaaS Services is often referred as PaaS.

- Providing managed Cloud infrastructure and application services on top of IaaS or PaaS, including all services (maintenance, support, and upgrades) is also referred to as SaaS, whether single or multitenant.

These main delivery models are explained in detail in the following sections.

2.3.1 Delivery Models and Share of Responsibility

As introduced above, the main difference in Cloud delivery models is the elements or levels of the technology stack and the degree of responsibility users have over those components. As a consumer of Cloud services, position yourself or your organization as a customer or consumer so you are responsible for managing and maintaining the activities included within the delivery models you provision and use, as shown on figure 2.9 no matter whether your company might be using a third-party host, outsourcer, or service provider that is doing it for you.

With Cloud models, the responsibilities of the Cloud vendors require many activities (often automated) that are already part of the pricing and billing of the Cloud elements you consume.

For those non-techies, there is a very popular analogy created by Albert Barron of IBM to explain the different delivery models with distinct ways of consuming pizza. Look at Pizza as a Service, as you can see in figure 2.10.

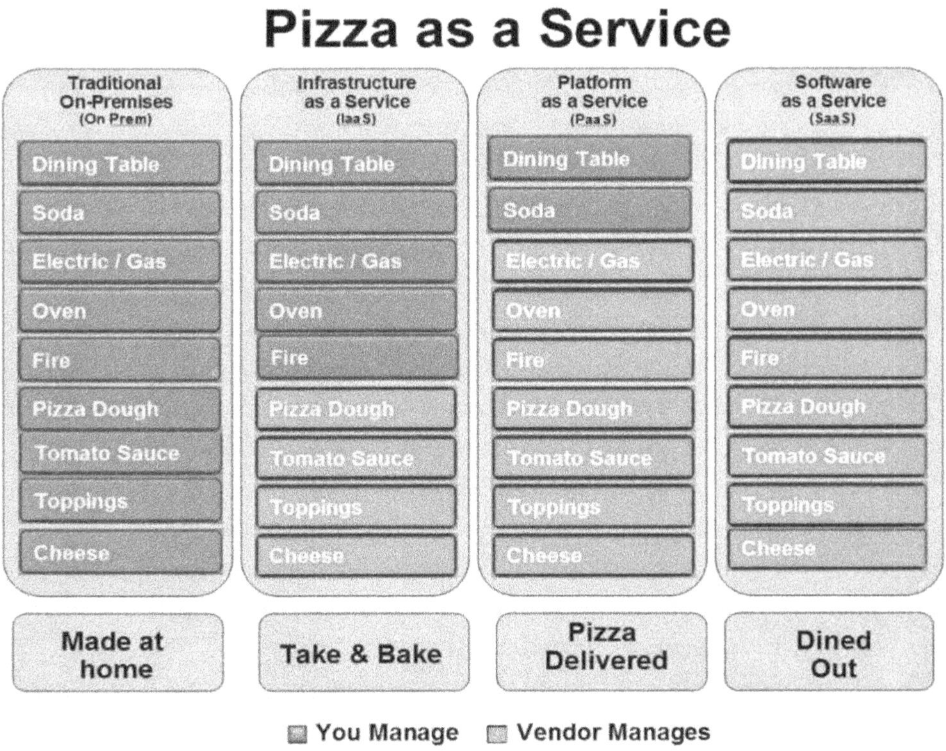

Pizza as a Service

Traditional On-Premises (On Prem)	Infrastructure as a Service (IaaS)	Platform as a Service (PaaS)	Software as a Service (SaaS)
Dining Table	Dining Table	Dining Table	Dining Table
Soda	Soda	Soda	Soda
Electric / Gas	Electric / Gas	Electric / Gas	Electric / Gas
Oven	Oven	Oven	Oven
Fire	Fire	Fire	Fire
Pizza Dough	Pizza Dough	Pizza Dough	Pizza Dough
Tomato Sauce	Tomato Sauce	Tomato Sauce	Tomato Sauce
Toppings	Toppings	Toppings	Toppings
Cheese	Cheese	Cheese	Cheese
Made at home	**Take & Bake**	**Pizza Delivered**	**Dined Out**

■ You Manage   ▨ Vendor Manages

Figure 2.10 – Pizza as a Service

2.3.2   IaaS—Infrastructure as a Service

NIST defines Infrastructure as a Service (IaaS) like this: The capability provided to the consumer to provision processing, storage, networks, and other fundamental computing resources where the consumer is able to deploy and run arbitrary software, which can include operating systems and applications. The consumer does not manage or control the underlying Cloud infrastructure but has control over operating systems, storage, deployed applications, and possibly limited control of select networking components (e.g., host firewalls).

IaaS is basically representing the underlying hardware resources such as networking, storage (e.g., disks or backup space), and computer resources (CPUs or memory).

Note: When deploying IaaS in well-known Public Clouds such as

Azure, AWS, or GCP, you always select a supported operating system (either most flavors of Linux or a Windows Server). Although the Cloud vendor provides the operating system, you, as customer or consumer, are responsible for maintaining it.

Although the Cloud portals can be used as very easy wizards to provision IaaS resources, usually these tasks are automated via scripting languages. Now Cloud system administrators and design architects have to develop skills to provision, configure, manage, and update the IaaS resources and other related Cloud elements that might be required. Detailed information on design and deployment in the Cloud can be found in chapter 2 of the second volume of this book.

Although it might well happen that in the upcoming years SaaS and PaaS will mostly overtake IaaS. From the beginning of the Public Cloud offering, IaaS has been heavily used for many purposes and reasons. IaaS is the choice for running all that software and applications that would traditionally run on physical or virtual systems on premises, but with all the advantages and flexibility provided by the Cloud. Users, organizations, and enterprises are heavily consuming IaaS for mainly the following reasons:

- It is easy and quick to consume and set up (minutes versus days orweeks).
- There is flexibility for choosing and scaling according to requirements, with very low cost. With traditional on-premises IT, there is a need to at least do some capacity planning, while in the Cloud you can easily and quickly change or scale your resources.
- Users avoid technological obsolescence.
- Hardware resiliency in the Cloud is cheaper.
- The Cloud vendor handles support and hardware infrastructure operations directly.
- Public Cloud vendors invest a lot in security and compliance certifications; therefore they come with lots of standard security and compliance features, which companies would find otherwise difficult, costly, or nearly impossible to set up to the same level.

2.3.3   PaaS—Platform as a Service

NIST defines PaaS as the capability provided to the consumer to deploy consumer-created or acquired applications created using programming languages, libraries, services, and tools supported by the provider onto the Cloud infrastructure. The consumer does not manage or control the underlying Cloud infrastructure, including networks, servers, operating systems, or storage, but has control over the deployed applications and possibly the configuration settings for the application-hosting environment.

PaaS is a Cloud-based computing environment designed to support the rapid development, running, and management of applications. It is integrated and abstracted from lower-level infrastructure components.

When using PaaS Cloud resources, the Cloud service provider is responsible for provisioning and managing the lower-level infrastructure resources and for providing a fully managed application development and deployment platform. PaaS provides developers with the appropriate flavors of operating systems, databases, middleware, software tools, and managed services, usually in a multitenant environment.

The biggest added value of PaaS is that the Cloud provider fully manages these Cloud servers, so developers are completely abstracted from the lower-level details of the environment and do not have to worry about things like managing or upgrading the scalability or security needs of the underlying platform.

There are two basic integration points that any PaaS solution has to support:

- Integration with the underlying IaaS makes it seamless for developers to get access to hardware resources. Developers don't need to concern themselves with the where and how these resources are provisioned. They just let the PaaS do it for them. Usually such integration is accomplished through APIs that the IaaS stack makes available to the PaaS vendors.
- The second integration point is with the SaaS layer or application vendors that want to develop value-added generic functional services and make them available for developers to consume in an on-demand

manner. This is usually accomplished by PaaS supporting a variety of runtimes that applications can be deployed in and a marketplace or catalog where these services can be published for consumption.

Some of the PaaS vendors use open-source platforms like Cloud Foundry while other vendors have a more proprietary implementation. An open-source implementation may have the benefits of portability, whereas a vendor-specific offering may have a better support model. Enterprises should evaluate these considerations before picking a PaaS strategy.

Public Cloud includes a marketplace for quick and instant deployment of PaaS services and resources, and thousands of vendors are offering their PaaS services through these Cloud marketplaces, giving an unprecedented agility for users and enterprises to easily and quickly provision the most advanced tools for their application developments.

There are all types of PaaS resources in these marketplaces: managed databases development tools, AI, analytics, IoT, messaging systems, web platforms, and so many others. Figure 2.11 is a screenshot of the Microsoft Azure Marketplace, where you can see some of the PaaS services that can be provisioned.

PaaS Cloud services are very well suited for all type of developments, such as modern web or mobile applications that require automatic scalability. On top of that, current PaaS offerings, specifically in web development environments, are quite well coupled with modern DevOps tools.

In regards to adopting or migrating your systems and applications to PaaS, coming from on-premises environments, commonly there will be the need to rearchitect your applications. To make the most secure, performant, and cost-effective use of PaaS services, a good design is always required.

PaaS provides many benefits. In summary, it helps organizations to minimize operational costs and increase productivity through a quicker time to market.

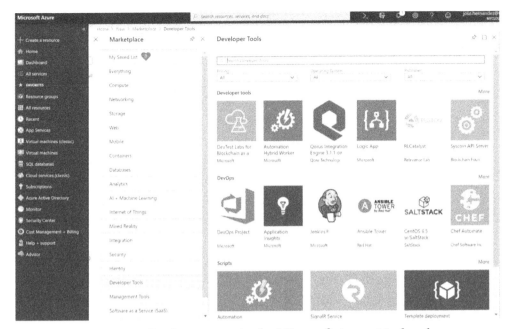

Figure 2.11 – PaaS resources in the Microsoft Azure Marketplace

2.3.4   SaaS—Software as a Service

NIST defines SaaS as "the capability provided to the consumer is to use the provider's applications running on a cloud infrastructure. The applications are accessible from various client devices through either a thin client interface, such as a web browser (e.g., web-based email), or a program interface. The consumer does not manage or control the underlying cloud infrastructure including network, servers, operating systems, storage, or even individual application capabilities, with the possible exception of limited user specific application configuration settings."

SaaS is the simple concept of having your full application running on someone else's data centers and had many predecessors, like application service provider (ASP) vendors did in the early days of the internet.

SaaS has been around for years, but some view the launch of Salesforce.com's CRM service in 1999 as a significant moment in SaaS's move into the mainstream. SaaS is the most common form of Cloud computing, where you use a browser and an internet link to access an application that's hosted and managed on servers in a service provider's data center. You pay for the service according to how much you use it or by subscription—rather than buying a license and paying for maintenance as you would with software run on premises. When people talk about on-demand software and hosted apps, they're usually talking about SaaS.

SaaS are fully managed applications in the Cloud. Users connect to these applications using any type of client or device, most commonly any type of web browser or mobile application client. Because of the way that SaaS services are developed and maintained, usually SaaS providers make the same Cloud-based services available on a multitude of clients and devices.

There are thousands of SaaS of all types available for immediate use and consumption, and we all have been using SaaS applications for a long time now, from productivity and collaboration tools such as Google Docs or Office365 or enterprise business software such as NetSuite, SuccessFactors, Microsoft Dynamics, Workday, and so on. In fact, most of the apps we use from our smart devices are a form of SaaS. We have been using them now for years.

SaaS is the Cloud delivery model that offers the most advantages to both users and enterprises, but of course, it´s not always the answer for every organization´s specific needs.

2.3.5 Cloud Strategies and Deciding for the Right Delivery Models

As introduced in the first chapter of this book, many organizations have decided for an all-Cloud or a Cloud-first strategy. In short, it means:

- A Cloud application or resource should cover any new business requirement. A SaaS application is preferred. If not possible or available, then go for a PaaS environment for developing specific processes. And lastly, if there is a short way for covering requirements with utilities, tools, or software available on top of VMs, then IaaS is selected.
- Every legacy system and application that can be moved to the Cloud will be migrated, if feasible and cost-effective.

Business requirements and availability of the right solution, architecture and support structure, and an appropriate Cloud governance will provide the answer for which one to choose, which of course can be a combination of several. You are not restricted to just SaaS or IaaS; however, some careful planning and design must be considered since integrating different Clouds. (For example, having VM on Google Cloud or AWS and a SaaS application provided by Microsoft or SAP has some technical challenges that have to be addressed.)

Let's review the reasons and advantages for selecting any of the Cloud delivery models. Reasons that apply to all three main Cloud delivery models include:

- All Cloud delivery models (offered "as a service") are considered a service cost, thus an operational expense (OPEX) and not a capital expenditure (CAPEX)
- You don't have to spend a one-time, up-front big infrastructure, platform, or software license, so the barrier for having the best applications is much lower than with on-premises systems.
- Strategically all Cloud solutions enable to expand your markets quicker, easier, and cheaper. You could open a new office or subsidiary, and you can have the solution ready for your users just by having internet access.
- You have more flexibility for growth, and it enables better and quicker innovation for companies.
- Extended security in data centers of the Public Cloud comply with security standards certifications that would cost millions for private customers to have in their own data centers. Data travels are encrypted.
- There is anywhere, any time, and mostly any device access.

The common reasons for selecting PaaS or SaaS include:

- **IT Operations Convenience:**

  - There's no need to spend time for selecting the servers, storage, and specific IT platforms (operating systems, databases engines, and application servers) for your applications.

- There's no need for installing your hardware, software, platform, and applications components and no need to install patches for the firmware or the software.
- There's no need for selecting and installing your backup hardware and software for your applications, neither for testing them.
- PaaS and SaaS vendors will (should) adapt to your growing and shrinking application needs, whether it might be in terms of supporting fewer or additional users or providing less or additional computing power to meet the agreed SLAs.
- Overall, both with PaaS and SaaS, your IT infrastructure is highly simplified. There's no need for extra data center space and no energy consumption or additional related costs.

– **Maintenance Reasons**

- Your PaaS or SaaS providers handles solving bugs (software errors) and installing patches and updates.
- New releases and maintenance fees are included in your billing or subscription.
- Your SaaS provider must observe the SLAs with you.
- Scalability was never easier.
- SaaS vendors guarantee that their multitenancy approach will never allow a company to access another's company data or information.

SaaS solutions can be the choice for you or your company as long as

- You can find the right SaaS solution for your business and application requirements, including your critical business processes. Or the SaaS solution allows for enhancing and developing your specific critical business needs.
- There is economic sense (savings, clear return on investment, or time for current asset amortization is due) for the adoption or migration to SaaS.
- Business risks for adoption or migration are low or very low.

So if there is a good SaaS solution for your critical business needs, it makes economic sense, and migrating or adopting the solution involves little risk, then SaaS solutions are a very option. Let's see a few reasons why to select SaaS.

- SaaS implementation projects are cheaper because 25 to 40 percent of tasks, especially on the technical side, are not required.
- When you subscribe to a SaaS application, you already have the infrastructure included and often the platform (PaaS) for enhancements and development.
- Disaster recovery (DR) generally comes "in the SaaS deal" by default, so there's no need to engage a DR consulting project and to contract or test a DR site.
- Your Saas vendor performs system monitoring.
- There's no need to have a physical shelfware system in place to organize your software kits.
- There's no need for having a landscape of servers for quality, testing, integration, or pre-production systems.
- Often SaaS vendors provide for an easy and quick way of having a complete test system, a copy of your production system, by the click of a button in the SaaS application.
- Your SaaS vendor has to provide excellent customer service at all times to avoid having unsatisfied customers and increased churn rate. They cannot just "sell and go."
- There are no maintenance fees. (They are included in the subscription fees.)
- Your minor or major maintenance or upgrade projects are significantly smaller and thus less time-consuming than traditional on-premises software.
- You are not tightening to the traditional product release software models.
- In SaaS, system admin tasks are usually fewer in number. They are also simpler and less time-consuming.
- Your software releases are always current.
- Business continuity is better guaranteed in big SaaS vendors that have distributed data centers in diverse geographies or around the world, which can react to DR in an automated fashion.

- SaaS vendors provide single sign-on mechanisms to integrate SaaS and on-premises applications (Hybrid Clouds).
- Organizations regularly audit SaaS providers to ensure they meet the necessary security standards.
- Training and enablement are usually quicker and cheaper.
- SaaS typically provides a much richer user experience.
- With SaaS, including or integrating external and public web services is typically faster and easier than with on-premises apps.
- Personalizing SaaS is easier and often with no need for programming.
- Most SaaS providers include some type of application or solution store with add-on solutions and enhancements by the vendor and its partners that can be directly tested and deployed online.
- SaaS solutions are better prepared for mobility, and often mobile solutions are included in your subscription.
- It is easier to get new functionality faster.
- There is increased user productivity.
- Audit and compliance of SaaS applications must be provided out of the box.
- Being in the web, your SaaS applications can benefit from real-time information; thus you are better informed for taking decisions.
- Merger and acquisitions are technologically easier.
- SaaS applications are much better for extended collaboration among businesses and customers.
- There is flexibility and convenience for SaaS users. Browser use is common and widespread, so user adoption is generally faster than with on-premises.
- There is better communication and knowledge sharing.
- SaaS can increase your customer reach and provide a better or new customer experience.
- There is better application time to market and better solution time to value.
- There is lower overall TCO.

In summary, any Cloud delivery model offers many benefits and reasons for selecting any of them for your business needs. It's a question of availability of your most specific requirements and architecting the right design to meet those needs.

2.4   Types of Clouds

Traditionally, as shown in figure 2.12, the types of Clouds that are commonly considered are Public, Private, Hybrid, and Community.

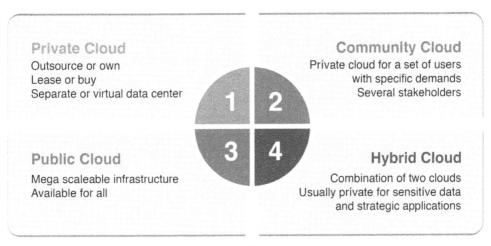

Figure 2.12 – Cloud Types

This is, however, a tricky issue for questioning, specifically if we want to contract whether each of those types are really meeting the definition and characteristics of Cloud as defined by NIST. Let's have a closer look at each of those types.

2.4.1   Public Cloud

The Public Cloud is made up of computing resources and services provided by a Cloud vendor, based on the standard Cloud computing model, offered through the public internet, and available to the general public that wants to consume it. In practice, a Public Cloud must meet the criteria for the computing model characteristics:

*   scalability and elasticity (providing the impression of unlimited resources)

- on-demand self-service (no need for anyone in the Cloud vendor to perform any manual action)
- Pay per use
  - o It must be observed that different Public Cloud vendors offer several types of pay per use, for example, billing by strict consumption by the second, reserved instances, burst instances, subscription based, and many more. It´s not easy to understand billing by Public Cloud vendors, so it´s important to comprehend as much as possible since this issue, together with workload optimization, can make the whole difference in cost savings as compared with traditional on-premises. An example of how to estimate costs for the Azure Cloud service is shown in figure 2.13, using the Azure Price calculator.

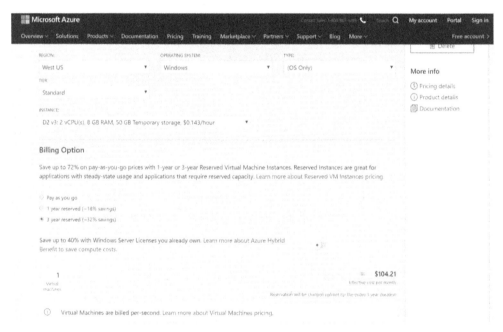

Figure 2.13 – Microsoft Azure Price Calculator

- Resource pooling or multitenancy (ensuring that there is separation of the resources that different users or organizations are using)

While some of the largest Public Cloud vendors such as Amazon Web

Services (AWS), Microsoft Azure, Google Cloud Platform, or Alibaba offer a large number of Cloud resources and services mostly based on IaaS and PaaS, other large Cloud vendors such as Salesforce.com, SAP, or Workday offer mostly SaaS and PaaS. Well-known services like Dropbox offer Storage as a Service (IaaS).

2.4.2 Private Clouds

In a Private Cloud, a single organization owns or leases the IT resources, and the owner of this infrastructure or a managed service provider maintains it. The computing facilities can be located at the organization's own data center or at a third party, and these resources are normally located behind a corporate firewall.

The first issue that must be considered is if there is such a thing as a Private Cloud when looking at the degree of compliance with the features and characteristics of Cloud as defined by NIST.

- Resources are not as scalable as in the Public Cloud, so there is no sense of unlimited resources.
- Pay per use is not the case since the organization has either procured or leased all the computing infrastructure.
- On-demand self-service can be achieved and even automated in Private Clouds, but always considering the limitations of the resources, so it might happen that a Cloud service or resource is not available.
- Resource pooling is also possible in Private Clouds, but unless the underlying computing technology is a real Cloud stack, mostly Private Cloud providers only use either virtualization technologies and containers.

There are vendors and open-source organizations offering real Private Cloud technology stacks, the most well-known being OpenStack and Microsoft Azure Stack. As for the decision on adopting or migrating to the Private or Public Cloud, there are several topics and requirements to be considered, which is discussed in the next section.

Because of the emergence and strength of Cloud adoption, many traditional hosting and outsourcing data centers are somehow confusing the users and changing their names as Cloud centers, but when confronted with the actual features and engineering that Cloud computing provides, they are not real Cloud. So what is the difference between data center and Cloud?

A data center can be defined as a facility that incorporates components such as servers, communication media, and data storage facilities. Along with this, it also contains various components that are essential to run a data center like power supply, backup systems, redundant communication connection, security devices, and so on. It's an on-premises hardware solution where all the resources are locally present at access, which is in-house providers typically run and maintain.

A Cloud is a virtual infrastructure that is accessed or delivered with a local network or accesses the remote location through internet. The Cloud services can be accessed on-demand whenever the user requires on a pay-per-use basis or a dedicated resource. This model is known as IaaS. Within this environment, the user can access computing resources, networking services, and storage, which the users can access on-demand without any requirement of physical infrastructure. It is an off-premises form of computing that can be accessed from the internet. A third party maintains and controls its maintenance and updates.

In the following section, we discuss extensively the main differences and issues between on-premises and Cloud, with some real-life examples of those differences.

2.4.3   Community Cloud

A Community Cloud can be considered a variant of Private Clouds, but in this case, a group of companies or organizations with a common concern or business share or own the infrastructure of a Cloud resource. Or it could be even that a group of companies want to build their own Cloud to share the costs of building and operating it.

This type of Cloud is the less common and widespread of all types of Cloud and uncommon for the general public and most companies; however, it is being used in organizations of public and education nature, like universities, research centers, and the like.

Adopting or migrating to this type of Cloud would be a similar process to those adopting real Private Cloud models.

2.4.4   Hybrid Cloud

A Hybrid Cloud is referred to as the combination of on-premises data centers or Private Clouds with a Public Cloud. By combination, we are meaning seamless connectivity. A different issue we cover later is how seamless the integration can be. So the requirements to build a Hybrid Cloud would be:

- You must be using at least a Public Cloud, such as Microsoft Azure, AWS, Alibaba, or Google Cloud Platform.
- You have on-premises systems, either your own, hosted, or a Private Cloud platform.
- Networking connectivity exists between these environments.

Since organizations don't have much control over the actual configuration of Public Clouds, they have to make sure to design their on-premises or Private Cloud architectures and connectivity to be compatible and accessible.

We prefer to distinguish between two types of Hybrid Clouds.

- The most common Hybrid Model is the one that combines on-premises data centers with Public Clouds. In this model, the main design issues are connectivity and security, while real actual integration for access control, identity management, provisioning, and managing the full landscape has to be solved with different tooling and general scope management and operations software. Additionally migrating systems from Private to Public would require specific tooling able to convert between image formats.
- The pure Hybrid Cloud model is the one made by the combination of the same underlying Cloud computing technology (although not exactly the same services), like Microsoft Public Azure and AzureStack or Private and Public OpenStack-based Clouds. The main difference and advantages of this model is that they both use real

native integration and can use exactly the same tools for managing and provisioning services.[3]

The underlying format of the virtual instances is the same; therefore moving services or migrating between Private and Public is native and straightforward.

In either case, Hybrid Cloud implementation provides many benefits, and it's a logical step in the enterprise journey to the Cloud.

- The first main advantage is keeping use of the systems and applications that are running on premises and cannot—or are not to—be moved or replaced in the short time, either for technical or economic reasons.
- For companies located in countries or regions that have strict compliance regulations and require their data within their country boundaries, they need to keep this data within the local on-premises data centers while they start using Public Clouds for those systems that do not need those compliance requirements.
- Legacy systems are still running applications that are both critical and important for the companies and cannot be technically migrated to the Public Cloud. They need to stay on premises and still have a good level of integration with other systems located in the Public Clouds.
- When the capital investments in infrastructure and licensing is still being amortized, it makes economic sense to keep certain systems on premises and be moving them as they lose their value.
- It's currently even possible to keep hosting critical business systems on premises and use the Public Cloud for peak loads for those same systems as extra computing resources and then release them when they are no longer needed.
- Certain type of systems that require very low latency might not be good candidates for immediate migration to the Cloud, like real-time systems located near production lines or trading systems.

[3] The physical finite limitations of the Private Cloud make that not all hyperscalable services and resources available in the Public Cloud would be available in the Private one.

There are can be some benefits in the Hybrid Cloud models, but for the common model, there are also some technical and organizational challenges.

- As stated above, solid network connectivity and security must be well designed and managed.
- IT governance will include both traditional IT on-premises policies and procedures, and additionally you have to include the needs for governing your Cloud resources. This includes that operating, monitoring, and managing the whole ecosystem is more complex in this type of environment.
- You might need different tooling to operate the whole landscape, one that is able to both manage on-premises and Cloud systems, for example, your backup solution, VPN solutions, alerting systems, and so on.
- Your SLAs must adapt to the different environments.
- Setting up identity management and a single sign-on hybrid environment can be more complex than in either pure Hybrid or pure Public Cloud scenarios.

2.5 Deciding between Cloud Types: On-Premises/ Private vs. Public Cloud

As IT, the main priority is to provide solutions to run the business processes of their organizations. In most technology issues, no one suit fits all, so different IT organizations might approach a Cloud type (or keep certain systems on premises) and delivery model decision considering their own requirements and variables.

When confronted with making technology decisions for the organizations, there are some common variables for any choice to be made, like costs, compliance, security, availability of the required services, infrastructure and applications, existing ecosystem, and the timing of the business requiring modernization.

Let's look at what the differences are as well as some examples when choosing the Cloud type for your business requirements, considering that common Private Clouds are often equivalent to on-premises systems. The differences between pure Private Clouds has been already introduced earlier.

2.5.1 Differences between On-Premises IT and Cloud IT

The following table includes a summary categorized by different levels or criteria.

Criteria	On Premises	On the Cloud
Cost	You pay for all infrastructure you have, no matter if you use them or not.	You pay only for the computing capacity you need at any time. There are also offers (discounts) for predefined capacities.
Control	You have full control of what you want for your data center.	You have very limited control of your infrastructure.
Elasticity	You have to dedicate lots of efforts to design the hardware needed. You have calculated the peak capacity needed, maybe with insufficient information. Add a reasonable margin, monitor constantly, and pay for all of it.	You start with some services and add some automatic rules for scalability. The Cloud will scale up and down your resources, using just the needed resources for the load. Capacity planning is not practically needed.
More cost-related aspects	This includes space, electricity, refrigeration, cameras, security, security personnel, insurance, and fire-extinguishing. You usually forget about these hidden costs, unless you are the one who pays for them.	These costs are zero in the Cloud, or you can consider that those are included within any service you provision.

Security	You have to provide your own level of security (physical, logical, personnel, and procedures). You then depend only on these measures.	You depend on an external provider (Cloud provider) for security. You have to consider if this security is better than the one you have on premises. Can a thief go inside your data center?
Scalability	Scalability is limited and costly.	In practical terms, the Public Clouds provide a sensation of infinite scalability.
Capacity planning	This is required in order to meet demands.	There is only basic capacity planning since it's easy and quick to adjust the supply of resources to the demands.
Availability (time to market)	You need a lot of time (administration, procurement, and paperwork) to get new systems. Then it has to be checked, updated, have applications installed, and so on.	You get as many Cloud services (servers, platforms, software, or any other service) updated and provisioned almost immediately.
Create-and-forget	You have to take care of all services, hardware, and software and make sure no uncontrolled changes have been done.	You declare what services are needed and their relationships in a declarative form, and the Cloud will make sure all the services are there.

Obsolescence	A common situation includes some operating system, app, and firmware that the manufacturer no longer supports. You can no longer update it, have support for it, or install security patches.	The Cloud automatically offers the newest technologies and updates the services accordingly.
Technical knowledge in your team	You have to know skilled people in your team for every possible aspect (operating system, communications, security, database, dev, etc.).	Your team must know the basic Cloud technologies but then concentrate on their job.
Latest technologies	Some of the newest apps (AI, machine learning, IoT, etc.) are no longer developed for on-premises environments.	These new technologies are only deployed in the Cloud because of their requirements. If you want to work with these technologies, you have to know the Cloud.
Inventory (and cost)	You can't see all the computers, as they are scattered across many sites, data centers, and subnets. Inventory is usually partial.	All your services are reachable from the same place, using the same API. Getting a full inventory is straightforward.
Computers left uncontrolled		It's very easy to create services (for any reason but especially tests) and leave them on. This will affect your bill! Note the importance of automation and monitoring as well as creating the environments using a formal process, a declarative way.

Divide and conquer	When you need a service (e.g., a hardware comms device), you have to buy one that is big enough for your load. This leads to more monolithic solutions.	Thanks to Cloud scalability, you can get several smaller services instead of a big one for a lesser cost. Each one will scale independently. You can get, for example, its cost divided by cost center. Of course automation will help manage a bigger number of smaller services.
Automation	Everything can be automated, but traditionally it was not done.	Everything can be automated. Being a new approach, all new services are deployed (and monitored and managed) using automation from the beginning.
Training	Your team already knows everything, and sometimes you provide training about newer versions of old services or training only to new employees.	Your team has to be trained on many new aspects, all the services now running in the Cloud. You have also to know automation to some degree.
Employee motivation	Employees keep on focusing on the old problems, with no time to learn new technologies. In the end, you get an obsoleted, unmotivated team.	Your employees can concentrate on the top-of-the-wave technologies.

Table 2.1 - Differences between On-Premises IT and Cloud IT

2.6   Reasons and Drivers for Moving to Cloud

Business managers are always looking for applications to help them run their businesses more efficiently—whether it's for analyzing data for faster decision-making or getting greater visibility into business operations.

And whether those capabilities come from commercial or customized apps, the burden is on IT to deliver and operate an ever-expanding set of services under continuous budget pressure.

There are many reasons for Cloud adoption, looking at them from different angles. Many of the reasons are economic in nature, such as cost reduction, leveraging OPEX for IT resources, and pay per use. Others have to do with the fact that implicit externalization of a big deal of operations and automation provides a high strategic value. Let's look at some of the most important ones since the advantages of different Cloud delivery models and types have been already broadly introduced in earlier sections.

- *Enterprise agility.* This is defined as the capacity and velocity for enterprises to adapt to changes, which means that business organizations can now adapt to changes and react in a much quicker and more flexible way. This is probably the single most important reason for Cloud adoption since in a fast-changing world, being able to adapt and find competitive advantage in their markets is of paramount importance.
- *Innovation capability.* Cloud computing allows companies to design, develop, and test new ideas, products, solutions, and services faster and with much lower entrance costs.
- *Avoidance of IT infrastructure capacity planning.* For a long time, especially for midsize to large enterprises, there was a recurrent need for performing lengthy and often costly capacity planning consulting projects. Capacity was—and is—a critical aspect for most, if not all, companies, taking into consideration that technology is critical for supporting most companies' processes. However, with the hyperscalability and elasticity offered by Cloud computing, capacity planning, although necessary for budgeting reasons, is not as critical and as costly as it is with traditional IT since the impression of infinite resources of the Cloud allows for consuming and paying for what is really needed and used. This is a very key aspect of Cloud versus legacy IT operations and often not considered by those still resisting the Cloud when doing the business case.

- *Time to market, time to value.* This is quicker projects with faster value. The implicit nature of the Cloud services—with capacity for self-service and immediate provisioning (seconds, minutes, hours, etc.) of infrastructure, platforms, and applications—projects to support business needs can start and finish faster. The lower cost of immediate services renting instead of the more complex and slower buying processes makes computing resources more affordable, accelerating the time required for deployment and implementation of systems and applications.

- *Social and collaboration capacity.* More than ever, the relationship with the business partners (customers, vendors, logistics, etc.) is bidirectional, and most enterprises are increasingly adopting a customer-centric business strategy instead of a product-centric one. This reinforces the need for active and multichannel collaboration and communication, which the internet and Cloud computing have greatly enabled.

- *Auto-scalable managed services.* Although it might not apply to all types of businesses, the capacity of the Public Cloud providers to auto-scale up or down services based on different type of metrics (e.g., average CPU consumption, hits per second, etc.) provides enterprises, in particular, those with a 24/7 exposition to customers through the internet (e-commerce/online shopping sites) the ability to match the demand in peaks and valleys of activity.

Needless to say, there are many more reasons and advantages for adopting or moving to Cloud. We just wanted to mention those more relevant with business itself. Altogether we can see that Cloud computing is a strategic capacity that enables a business model's transformation of companies in ever-changing economic and social changes. What has been the buzz of the last few years: digital transformation? We do consider that Cloud computing is the technological pillar for that.

2.6.1 Reasons for Not Moving to Cloud Computing

Cloud computing is great, but it is not a silver bullet for every organization's needs. And besides the challenges for adopting or migrating to Cloud, there are also compelling reasons that might avoid, at least temporarily, for moving some of your systems and applications to the Cloud. For years and quite often, there has been resistance to change and the Cloud, especially by IT departments, and often as well, there were more excuses and fears than actual reasons.

Let's review several of the most important reasons that companies might postpone, think of a very detailed plan, or wait for the right Cloud resource to be available and tested.

- **Availability of software and applications for the available Cloud infrastructure**. Currently most of the application software is being developed for the Cloud and just for the Cloud. However, there are millions of both standard and custom-developed software and applications that were not and are not yet available for Cloud. If you have such application and are not planning to invest in refactoring or acquiring new Cloud-ready software, then those apps and systems have to remain on premises. This is particularly the case of software running on legacy platforms (operating systems and/or databases) that are not supported in Public Clouds.
- **Network latency**. Although there have been tremendous advances in network connectivity and capacity, there are sites and regions in the world that do not have access to fast networking and systems that, because of their nature, require a very low latency, which might not be the case when using Public Clouds. For this type of requirements, like real-time applications, possibly having on-site and on-premises systems are still the best choice
- **Highly critical business systems.** For different reasons, might happen that some highly critical systems are not -or not yet- supported in the Cloud. Sometimes it is a technical reason, like running only on mainframes, but not just a technical reason, but that the software and application vendor does not certify or provide support for its software in the Cloud. Or the combination of other technical reasons, like latency required to run this type of systems.
- **Compliance.** For those highly regulated companies or those whose legal compliance policies require that data does not leave the country or they need to comply with some type of compliance or security

certification, if this Cloud provider does not support your certification, then most probably this system should not be moved to the Public Cloud. However, this is a scenario for Private Clouds (either common or pure, as long as they are located within the boundaries allowed by your compliance regulations).

- **Security**. Reason or excuse? Actually security features provided in the Public Clouds are by far more advanced than those found in on-premises systems. Unless you or your organization do not transact with any business partner through the web and your systems need to be completely isolated from the outside world, security should not be a reason not to move to the Cloud. Needless to say, you need to care and implement your security policies, whether on premises or in the Cloud. Chapter 5 discuss security in the Cloud in great detail.

2.6.2   Risks of Not Moving to the Cloud

Sometimes we think that Cloud computing has created a very large, huge mess in the industry and business alike! Everybody seems to be loving it, but there is much more resistance in the IT industry to make it a big push, although this resistance is diminishing in giant steps and falling like the pieces of a domino.

We think that the general IT industry push for Cloud is because overwhelming customer demand forces them. If there are significant cost-saving reasons for moving to the Cloud, it means that someone is also losing part of their business. We have seen a lot of negative marketing against Cloud that, from our viewpoint, was somehow biased toward their own business.

Although there are thousands of companies and public institutions that have started the journey to the Cloud, the overall spending in Cloud IT is still in its adolescence, and according to analysts, in 2019, it is still around 12 to 15 percent of overall IT spending. Enterprises resisting the Cloud have both real technical reasons for doing so as well as excuses, leaving the line between reasons and excuses as a very fuzzy one.

Whether Cloud computing already represents 10 or 25 percent (depending on the analyst figures you read) at the end of 2020, all of them agree on the unstoppable rise of growth for the next few years, and overall Cloud spending might well surpass $500 billion (USD) by 2020, and all analysts seem to agree that we are seeing the "end of the beginning" on Cloud transition, adoption, and migration.

Nobody said that the journey to the Cloud would be an easy one and would not be challenges ahead, but no more than the adoption of other innovative computing technologies, like it was the emergence of the web or the boom of the mobile and social applications.

Late Cloud adopters have to deal with several issues when starting their journey, like:

1. It's not easy or obvious to select and contract Cloud services (with the exception of some SaaS).
2. You must know how to migrate, manage, support, integrate, and implement Cloud services.

We tend to compare Cloud adoption in a similar fashion with the consumption of music or movies: there are still and will be vinyl records, CDs, and DVDs; however, most of the music and entertainment today is consumed in digital formats (MP3 and audio and video streaming). There will always be on-premises software and legacy applications, but today the majority of the software being developed is Cloud-ready and Cloud-enabled, especially when the world tends toward mobile, social, collaborative, analytics, IoT, and AI, just to name a few.

While adopting and transitioning to Cloud comes at a cost and with a degree of challenges and risks, there are too many reasons and potential benefits for resisting it. As we introduced in the previous chapter about the enterprise journey to Cloud and we discuss extensively in the second volume of this book, your organization will realize the many benefits of the Cloud when it reaches a maturity and optimization stage.

Not adopting Cloud computing within a company strategy might be quite risky as we have seen how many thousands, if not millions, of companies would fade away with the continuous evolution of industries and technologies.

We all seem to like amazing start-up companies that are born embracing 100 percent digital, social, mobile, and Cloud technologies and how in relatively short periods of time they are competing head to head against big incumbents as well as very often get ahead of them. Why? Because they are more agile, flexible, and faster. They listen better, have more intelligence, and provide better customer experience when dealing with them. They are more competitive and more prepared for fast changes.

In summary, there are some risks involved if not moving to Cloud computing, such as:

- loss of competitiveness
- very slow pace of innovation, if any
- obsolete technology/software
- still must spend on commodity costs and CAPEX, which is less capital for other strategic investments
- slower market penetration
- much more effort, resources, and costs for solution rollouts
- capacity planning

Most companies either already know or are quickly becoming aware that they will have to adopt or move to the Cloud, and one compelling reason is that the software they need for running their business only works in the Cloud, which is going to become increasingly common.

Several analysts' research indicates that by 2020, only 5 percent of all applications will be still developed for on-premises systems. In the Public Cloud, all platforms are being quite standardized, so they are either Windows- or Linux-based systems. If you are a software company with the aim of selling your products to the broadest market, will you still develop for legacy systems?

2.6.3   When Is the Right Time for Moving to Cloud

In short: yesterday! Not being too radical: as soon as possible. There are some specific triggers that can help your organization take the decision to do so, in a practical way, "when a compelling event that creates the need and the opportunity," like, for example:

- end of the amortization of current IT investments
- renewal of your outsourcing, hosting, or maintenance contracts

- need for new systems and applications that can support new business processes
- end of the life cycle of any of your critical applications
- current running systems and applications that cannot adapt to new business models
- need to expand your markets, like opening new subsidiaries
- strategic decision to concentrate on the business and not in IT operations without any added value
- merger and acquisitions processes
- when confronted with difficult application integration projects
- when the company has decided to go all-digital

3 Types of Cloud Migrations

This chapter introduces multiple types and variants that can be found in enterprises when migrating to the Cloud. During this chapter, we are going to focus on the most common migration type classifications as well as the different technical options to migrate, how to move unsupported systems, and some examples. In a Cloud migration, there are other important things to consider that will be developed in the following chapters.

If you are a new start-up company that is going to directly use all your apps or your IT services using Cloud services, you are not really transitioning to Cloud, but adopting Cloud from the very beginning. There's no need for a transition, but there is need for some planning, design considerations, governance, security, and compliance factors to take into consideration.

In the case of companies that have been used to running their IT on traditional on-premises data centers (whether their own, hosted, or outsourced), there are several ways to transition to the Cloud.

1. Rip off a legacy application and start using a new contracted SaaS application that covers the business processes required. Besides common considerations, this type of transition would require data migration from the legacy application and possibly rebuild the interfaces with other applications, if any.
2. Migrate your infrastructure to the Cloud but leave the applications (whether standard software or custom developed) working as they are on your current data center. Here you are only substituting your on-premises infrastructure for a cloud IaaS. This is called rehosting.
3. Migrate your applications to the Cloud, changing your platform (operating system, database, development environment), for the same or compatible one in the Cloud. This process is a replatform.
4. Transform your applications to Cloud platform services, like databases and web applications.

5. Migrate your legacy software to a Cloud-enabled application, or Cloud modernization.

6. Implement the disaster recovery infrastructure for your on-premises applications in the Cloud.

7. Build a hybrid environment where some of your systems and applications are migrated or implemented on the Cloud and the rest of them remain on premises. One of the most common scenarios is a customer having the development, training, or testing environments in the Cloud and the production environments on premises.

8. Use Cloud storage for backup services, archiving, or content repositories.

The different ways of transitioning to the Cloud will be detailed in the following section.

3.1   Types of Cloud Migrations

There are many ways or types of migrations to move your current systems and applications to the Public Cloud, and while some of them are not actually pure migrations, there are common issues and challenges to consider. The tooling and technical procedures to perform the migration varies depending on the type of migration.

What migration option is better for the migration? This is one of the most important questions when facing a Cloud migration, and the answer could suppose the success or the failure of the migration project. The selection of the migration type and technique will be decided during or after the workload analysis phase and will depend on the following:

- **Technical restrictions:** source/target platform, desired end architecture, application requirements, integrations, networking issues, data gravity, security requisites, and so on
- **Business requirements:** maximum allowed downtime, timing, number of users, interfaces with other applications, application criticality, and so forth
- **Economic reasons:** migration tool cost, additional temporary infrastructure, migration project effort, and so on

Figure 3.1 shows the decision factors for the possible types of migrations to Cloud.

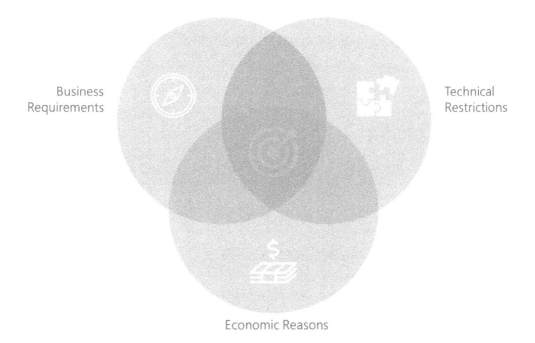

Figure 3.1 – Decision factors for type of Cloud Migration

There should always be two main drivers during any Cloud migration: reduce risks and minimize end-user impact. In this section, we will see how each type of Cloud migration requires different cost, effort, and time to be completed:

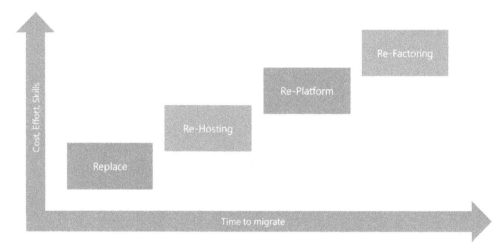

Figure 3.2 – Main Types of Cloud Migrations

3.1.1   Replace: Rip-off and Substitute

This type of migration consists in decommissioning an application and substituting it by a Cloud-based application, which can be SaaS or a new software on top of PaaS or IaaS. When changing to SaaS, the company outsources the new applications and IT services. While ripping off or decommissioning an application is not strictly a Cloud migration, there are important common aspects that need to be considered.

- Most probably the new application needs to be integrated, and it shares processes or data with other systems and apps.
- There might be the need to transfer the data from the old application to the new one. This would be a data migration process, which the target app or system usually provides. This process should be carefully made to avoid inconsistent data semantics.

When requirements for a business function change quickly and drastically, this approach avoids the time and investment of mobilizing a migration or development team. The main disadvantage is the loss of control, vendor lock-in, and possible lack of functionality in the new platform.

3.1.2   Revise: Upgrade to Cloud-Supported Release

Sometimes before performing a Cloud migration, it is required to update the application, operating system, or database to a Cloud-supported release or modify or extend the existing code base to support Cloud infrastructure. This should be done within your on-premises data center or use of a temporary location. After this, it should be performed one of the following migration types.

3.1.3   Rehosting (Lift-and-Shift)

This is the most basic approach to migrating applications to the Cloud, moving them without any code modification. The application changes the host to another hardware environment without any change in the application architecture. The company will have the same software that they have, but now in the Cloud.

Lift-and-shift migration is the more cost-effective migration. Rehosting is particularly effective in a large-scale enterprise migration. This Cloud migration can't take full advantage of the speed and versatility the Cloud can provide, as the application is using the same architecture as an on-premises one. In some cases, companies use this migration type as a first step in their Cloud transition journey. Once the systems are in the Cloud, it is easier to rearchitect and optimize the application.

This model is a good option for companies with a regular peak schedule and slow, predictable changes in their operations. The main driver when performing this migration is to reduce the company IT TCO. Some organizations have realized a cost savings of as much as 30 percent, without having to implement any Cloud-specific optimizations.

3.1.4   Replatform

The replatform type consists of migrating application to the Cloud with a small change on the underlying platform, such as the operating system. The database might change, and/or the database may be migrated to a managed instance, but still the application runs exactly in the same way that it did on premises. This is the most common case of some enterprise applications, such as SAP.

This approach offers a solid middle stage between rehosting and refactoring, allowing workloads to take advantage of basic Cloud functionality and cost optimization, without the level of investment required for refactoring.

In these migrations, it is very important to analyze and review that there aren't any complications related to the change of the platform: scripting, custom operating system or database developments, agents, installed third-party tools, and so on. Companies that need to have their application scalable, flexible, redundant, and available adopt this model.

3.1.5 Refactoring or Rearchitecting

This process could be the most time-consuming and resource-intensive type of migration. It consists of modifying the architecture and/or developing the same functionality for transitioning the application into Cloud native frameworks and services. With rearchitecting, the companies replicate the legacy application in the Cloud platform.

The new development could work in parallel with the legacy application during the process. The migration can be a partial or complete refactoring. In these migrations, the applications are migrated to PaaS services or moved into containers (containerizing). Refactoring could be a very complex and risky process, and some capabilities might be missing after migration.

3.2 Technical Migration Options

Each type of migration has several technical options to transfer and move the workloads and applications from on premises to the Cloud. There isn't one migration option that solves all scenarios and applications. As explained in the previous section, the technical procedure or solution should be selected depending on technical restrictions, business requirements, and economic reasons.

In the picture below, there is an example of all technical options available to migrate an SAP system to Azure Cloud depending only on the technical restrictions and characteristics of the source system.

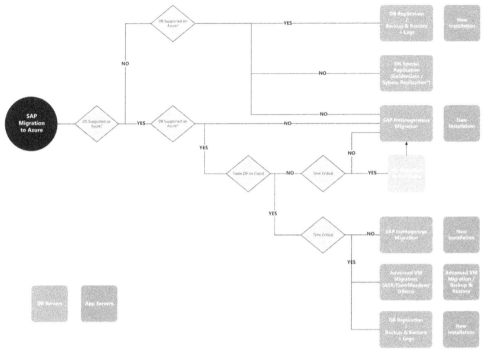

Figure 3.3 – SAP to Azure technical migration Decision tree

In this section, we will analyze some of the most common migration options: image/disk transfer, backup and restore, VM replication tools, database replication, export/import, disaster recovery, and containerizing.

	Replace	Revise	Rehosting	Replatform	Refactoring
Image/Disk Transfer		YES	YES		
Backup and Restore		YES	YES	YES	
VM Replication Tools		YES	YES		
Database Replication			YES	YES	

Disaster Recovery			YES	YES	
Export/Import			YES	YES	
Containerizing					YES

Table 3.1 - Migration option for each migration type

3.2.1   Image/Disks Transfer and Deployment

This is the simplest and less resource-intensive procedure of Cloud migration. This process only works for lift-and-shift migrations of virtualized environments.

In these cases, we take the hypervisor disks to transfer them from on premises to the Cloud. Next the VM will be deployed using the disks. All configuration and data are copied to the Cloud without any change. The main disadvantage is that during the whole process, there is a downtime in the systems.

It must be considered that sometimes Cloud agents should be installed before and/or after the migration. In some cases, before the migration, the hypervisor disks should be converted to a Cloud native format, for example. If a VM is hosted in a VMWare environment and should be moved to Azure, the disks should be converted from VMDK to VHD format.

3.2.2   Backup and Restore

This operation works in rehosting scenarios for machines and rehosting and replatform scenarios for databases. They can be very effective and safe. A target system must be previously deployed on the Cloud. Then a backup of the whole VM or database should be uploaded.

In this situation, some vendor tools (e.g., Veeam, Commvault, etc.) or database native functionality are often used to perform the backup and restore operations. Some of the available tools automates the backup/restore operations in order to reduce the resources to perform the required operations.

If you use a restore strategy of full backup and incremental backups, it is possible to significantly reduce downtime during the whole process.

3.2.3   Virtual Machine Replication Tools

There are many migration tools on the market that can support, simplify, and accelerate the migration to the Cloud. Normally they only work for rehosting (lift-and-shift), and most of them support converting VMs from different source and target hypervisors, for example, from VMware/ Hyper-V to AWS or to GCP and so on. Even from physical machines.

Some of these solutions have management consoles or accept scripting commands to orchestrate massive migrations. Others allow real-time replication to minimize downtime, migration time, or risks.

Depending on the replication technology, there are two main groups. Agent-based requires installing plug-ins or agents in the source VMs to perform migration operations. Agentless requires either access to the source hypervisor or admin credentials to the VM to be able to copy the VMs.

The disadvantages of the VM replication tools are that they do require access to the source and target networks and the license cost that they usually imply.

Some Public Cloud providers have in their service portfolio VM replication tools, such as Site Recovery (Azure) and Velostrata (Google Cloud Platform). Other tools very successful on the market are CloudEndure, Doubletake, Zerto, RiverMeadow, PlateSpin, and so forth.

3.2.4   Database Replication and DB Log Shipping

Database replication is one of the most common procedures when migrating a database. Database replication or mirroring uses procedures to replicate and copy databases in real time. Depending on the technical requirements and requisites, the change of operating system or the database server release could be achieved during the movement from the Cloud to on premises (replatform).

Databases usually have their own replication procedure (SQL Server – SQL Server Always On, SAP HANA – HANA Replication Services, Oracle Database – Oracle Data Guard, IBM DB2 – DB2 Replication Services, etc.). Or it could use a third-party replication tool (Golden Gate, SharePlex, etc.).

In these cases, migrations consist of replicating the database data into a previously installed empty cloud or PaaS database. Once all the data has replicated, to finish the migration, a failover on the replica should be performed.

Log shipping is very similar to database replication. This is the process of automating the backup of transaction log files onto a primary database server and then restoring them onto a secondary one. There are two main reason to choose log shipping over database replication: there are some technical limitations (number of replicas) and log retention. (If replication is disconnected, the primary database log file can fill up disk space and get blocked.)

3.2.5   Disaster Recovery

Some companies set up their disaster recovery systems in the Cloud as a middle stage in their migration process. There are some techniques (DB replication, log shipping, etc.) and tools (VM replication tools, DR solutions, etc.) that allow a company to replicate their production systems in the Cloud as a contingency site. Once the data is replicated and the company is confident that everything is working properly, it is possible to make a failover on the secondary site in the Cloud. This secondary site or replica will become the production environment, and the systems will be already migrated.

After this, the company has several options: keep their old on-premises site as a disaster recovery site, decommission the primary site and don't have a disaster recovery site, or decommission the primary site and build a new disaster recovery site in this Cloud or a different one.

3.2.6   Export / Import

Export/import procedures are another way of migrating databases. Most applications allow this procedure to be migrated. A copy of the database should be imported in a previously deployed database in the Cloud.

Some applications support heterogeneous migrations, meaning different combinations of operating systems and databases between the source and the target system, such as SAP solutions. This is done through an export with independent format, and this is a good choice for replatform type of migrations.

3.2.7   Containerizing

Containerizing an application is the process of making it able to run and deploy under containers. It is used on refactoring migrations.

A container is a standard unit of software that packages up code and all its dependencies so the application runs quickly and reliably from one computing environment to another, independently of the operating system, hypervisor, and hardware. Containers provide significant resource efficiencies compared to running applications directly on servers.

Not all the applications are technically prepared to be containerized. Most of the time, huge amounts of work and complex developments are required. Some companies are developing solutions and tools to automate this process.

3.3   How to Move Data to the Cloud

When a company is performing a Cloud migration, all data that resides on premises should be transferred to the target Cloud destination. This data movement could be one of the most critical tasks and can cause the failure of the migration project.

Just an example: let's suppose a customer needs to upload 5 terabytes of data (already compressed) to the Cloud. In its current data center, it has 100 Mbps available bandwidth. This customer will need more than six days, almost a week of downtime! Most companies cannot survive with their production systems shut down for one week.

In terms of data upload from its local data center to the Public Cloud, an enterprise has several options. These include the use of the public internet, a private/dedicated network connection, or an offline transfer. The type of data migration an enterprise chooses depends on the amount and type of data it wants to move, the required security, as well as how fast it needs to complete the migration.

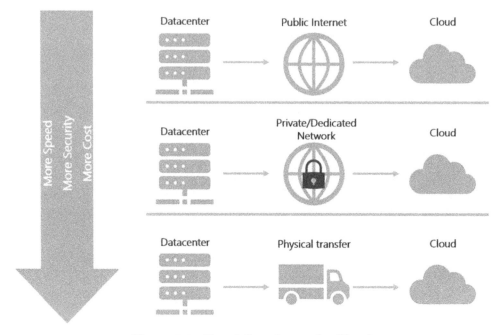

Figure 3.4 – Data Migration to the Cloud

3.3.1 Offline Transfer

When it is required to move massive amounts of data to the Cloud and a synchronous replication method is not available, the network transfer through public internet or private/dedicated network isn't an option because it supposes huge delays and downtime. Physical data transfer is the solution that guarantees more speed, performance, and security.

Most of the Cloud vendors offer offline data transfer devices that are shipped between the customer's site and the Cloud data center. Among others, AWS offers AWS SnowBall; Azure, Azure Data Box; GCP, Transfer Appliance; IBM Cloud, Mass Data Migration Service; Alibaba Cloud, Data Transport, and so forth.

3.4 What Applications and Systems Are Not Supported on Public Clouds

When we are facing a Cloud migration, there are systems that are not supported on Public Clouds. How do we identify these systems and applications? The most common scenarios where the systems are not supported on Public Clouds are indicated below. During the next section, we will see what to do with these systems.

3.4.1   Virtualization

Public Clouds are designed only for hosting virtualized environments. Although some vendors are including bare metal servers (IBM Cloud Bare Metal servers, Azure Large Instances, Amazon EC2 Bare Metal Instance, etc.) in their offering, this conflicts with one of the principles of Public Cloud: virtualization.

3.4.2   Operating System

All hyperscale Public Clouds have something in common: they only support 64-bit-based systems. In computer architecture, 64-bit or x64 computing is the use of processors that have data path widths, integer size, and memory address widths of sixty-four bits (eight octets). Also 64-bit computer architectures for central processing units (CPUs) and arithmetic logic units (ALUs) are those based on processor registers, address buses, or data buses of that size.

This means that only Windows Server (2003 and ahead) and Linux operating systems are supported on Public Clouds. Each Cloud provider has its own operating system support matrix, which is periodically updated in compliance with the operating system vendor. Additionally the following legacy operating systems are not supported on Public Clouds: HP-UX, IBM AIX, Sun Solaris, IBM AS/400, and so forth.

3.4.3   Technical Restrictions

There are several technical restrictions that must be considered when transitioning and migrating to Public Cloud. Among them, the most common ones are listed below.

3.4.3.1 Multicasting

In computer networking, multicast is group communication where data transmission is addressed to a group of destination computers simultaneously. Multicast is a technique for one-to-many or many-to-many communication.

Public Cloud networks are usually on a shared, virtual local area network (LAN or vLAN). The shared network and shared infrastructure are called a multitenant environment, like a multitenant apartment building. Allowing a "chatty" protocol inside a Cloud network could have a serious impact on the Cloud's performance.

For this reason, Public Cloud providers would rather disable UDP. Public Cloud doesn't have built-in hardware support for multicasting. Public Cloud customers also are not allowed to access the lower network layers, such as Layer 2.

3.4.3.2 Latency Restrictions

When any company is adopting Cloud computing, network bandwidth and latency issues are critical for some applications. There are several situations where Public Cloud is not valid due to latency and networking restrictions:

- Manufacturing Execution Systems (MES) that need almost zero latency to communicate
- Remote locations with poor connection
- High-precision systems that need to be close to the location (like drilling sites)

3.4.3.3 SMTP

Some Public Cloud providers don't allow installation of a SMTP service on a VM like you would run it on premises. One of the key issues here relates to the ephemeral nature of Cloud Public IP addresses and potential for abuse, along with the effects that it might have on other customers if they inherit your public IP addresses in the future. To solve this problem, it is necessary to install a SMTP server outside the Cloud or use PaaS or SaaS SMTP solutions.

3.4.3.4 Compliance Restrictions

Although it is technically feasible, some compliance issues don't permit moving the systems and the data to the Cloud.

3.4.3.5 Legal and Data Regulations

Some countries have specific regulations that forbid having some data outside the country, like personal, customer, and financial data. The data protection and privacy create tight controls on flows of personal data outside their respective countries through requirements such as data centers needing to be located inside each country.

For example, in Europe, General Data Protection Regulation (GDPR) doesn't allow hosting of personal and financial data outside the European Union. There are similar regulations in several countries around the world: the Australia Privacy Act, Japanese Personal Information Protection Act, and so forth.

3.4.3.6 Software Vendor Specifications

Some software vendors don't guarantee support when the systems are migrated to the Public Cloud or migrated under some combinations of Cloud vendor/operating system/database. Sometimes these decisions only respond to political motives or competition strategies among software companies. This is a common situation with enterprise software such as Oracle or SAP.

3.5 What to Do with Non-Supported Systems and Apps on the Cloud

As discussed in the previous point, some systems aren't supported on the Public Cloud. For these systems and applications, there are some possibilities when facing a Cloud migration.

3.5.1   Don't Migrate to the Cloud

Some applications and systems should be left in the source data center or migrated to a hosting or colocation center. The systems will remain as there were, and we only need to ensure connectivity and interfaces with the rest of the infrastructure. There are third-party companies that offer a colocation center close to Public Cloud vendors and guarantee SLA over connectivity and integrations.

3.5.2   Cloud Migration through Cloud Transformation

As seen in section 3.1, Types of Cloud Migrations, some forms of migration allow us to change the operating system. This could be used to transform the source system into a Cloud-supported version. Replace, replatform, and refactoring migrations accomplish these migrations. Some of the examples are the following:

- **Implementation of SaaS CRM solution** → Through replace strategies, some companies are getting rid of their old legacy CRM systems and adopting new SaaS CRM solutions. A data migration and interface reconfiguration are required.
- **Redevelopment of Fortran applications** → Most legacy applications, which have been developed some decades ago, are not supported in the Cloud. If you have a Fortran application, it may be redeveloped using Python or other Cloud-ready programming language and deployed on a web application or serverless PaaS service.
- **SAP Business Solutions heterogeneous migration** → Most SAP systems are working in platforms not supported in the Cloud (Oracle/ HP UX, Oracle/IBM AIX, DB2/AS400, etc.). Most companies are migrating and updating their SAP systems to SAP HANA database. Using SAP native heterogeneous migration procedure, it is possible to replatform the systems and move to the Cloud, SUSE operating system, and SAP HANA database at the same time.

3.6 Cloud Adoption Scenarios

The type of scenarios that enterprises can adopt or migrate to can be quite different depending on factors such as business objectives, the as-is status of systems and applications, external factors such as the availability of new technologies, services, functionalities, and others such as geographical location and legal and compliance regulations. As we have introduced earlier in this book, there is no one-suit-fits-all policy for Cloud adoption or migration.

Companies are already aware of the multiple benefits when migrating to the Cloud: lowering costs, the agility for having resource availability at scale and the fact of saving big initial investments can be summarized as the main benefit drivers.

However, defining and deciding what are the best options and scenarios for adoption for each type of business and its circumstances make selecting the right Cloud provider and services (or a combination of them) to be a very complex process.

3.6.1 Approach for Migrating Single Systems to the Cloud

When the migration of a single systems is required, it is first necessary to define which type of migration should be performed depending on the type of source system and the final status of the migration. For taking this decision, the available resources, the required project timelines, and technical parameters, among other parameters, must be taken into consideration.

Additionally, it is required to select which technical procedure or solution should be used to do the migration.

After the migration, it is always required to test the application, and in some cases, there are post-migration activities that should be done (interface reconfiguration, reinstallation of licenses, DNS changes, managed services, etc.).

3.6.2 Migrating a Full On-Premises Data Center to the Cloud

When you are facing a migration of a whole data center, the approach is similar to a single system migration, but it's going to be necessary to use a combination of migration types and procedures. The approach is the same but more complex because it is necessary to consider different elements: dependencies between systems and applications and logical grouping.

In integration aspects, the testing will be more complex. And designing the architecture should be done with a complete view of the technological landscape. The migration of a data center will be explained in more detail in the next chapters of the book.

3.6.3 Cloud Migration Scenario Examples

The number of models and scenarios are potentially unlimited, so we're just trying to describe a few of them, which are the ones we have found most often in customer Cloud migration projects. We will look at scenarios by looking at the following factors:

- strategy and business plans
- number and type of legacy applications
- current IT skills
- target markets
- agility and innovation drive
- usage and scalability needs
- legal, security, and compliance
- economic factors

As you will see in the following examples from the definitions of each company's unique environment and how those unique needs help define the priorities and strategy for technology adoption, there isn't a one-size-fits-all option for Cloud. Our belief is that for the next five to ten years, we're likely to see most companies with over two hundred employees using a hybrid set of Cloud-based solutions, which includes

Private, Public, Hybrid, and SaaS. Farther down the road, who knows? Maybe we'll get to the magical low-cost commodity cloud that will suit all.

Using the scenarios provided in this section as a model, you should be able to ascertain some of the critical decision factors in making a Cloud choice for your organization. Having a firm grip on what your teams are capable of, in combination with what a specific solution requires, will help you to better position IT as a partner instead of a roadblock.

3.6.4   Scenario 1—Seven Years Internet-Facing Midsize Enterprise

Company

An internet-facing midsize enterprise is a company with five hundred employees. Most of their business is driven through e-commerce and internet platforms. Its business has several peaks, and they are facing the competition of the worldwide online retailers, such as Amazon.

Migration Factors

Table 3.2 - Scenario 1 - Migration factors

Factor	Current State	Future State
Strategy	Losing market share	Need to gain competitive advantage against its competitors
Systems and apps	Around twenty apps, some of them already SaaS solutions	Cloud-first strategy decided in order to go to SaaS Some legacy can't be moved to Cloud.
Economics	Very limited investment capacity Need to reduce its IT costs	100 percent OPEX strategy

Legacy apps	Limited set of legacy applications	Active projects underway to retire all of them as opportunity provides
Staffing	Good-sized IT team focused on enabling an internet-driven business model	Focused on solutions that can scale at a manageable cost
Elasticity, geo-diversity, support structure	Primary applications are internet-facing, with each varying wildly in use depending on product launches and seasonal buying patterns.	Elasticity at scale is critical, along with an ability to rapidly deliver updates.
Agility	Agility is desired for competitive advantage.	Agility is measured in hours versus days and applies to the entire company.
Rapid growth, geo-distributed, internet-oriented	Business growth of 15 percent or more CAGR	Growth can be volatile and difficult to plan for.
Geo-distribution	Widely distributed workforce with developers and contributors in offices all over the world A customer base that is globally distributed and dynamic	Geodiversity is critical for application, performance, and fault tolerance.

Recommendations

In scenario 1, the primary usage characteristics for the company (global distribution, speed to market, and many locations for customers and staff/engineering) suggest that the focus should be put on utilizing Public Cloud for most solutions. If there are internal-focused applications that are fairly steady in their use, then the addition of Hybrid and/or Private

Cloud could make sense. Adoption of SaaS solutions will enable the required agility and flexibility for this company.

3.6.5 Scenario 2—Twenty-Five-Year-Old or More Large Multinational Enterprise

Company

A twenty-five-year-old or more large multinational enterprise is a company with more than five thousand employees. Critical and back-office processes are not internet-driven. It's losing market share due to its lack of agility against its competitors.

Migration Factors

Table 3.3 - Scenario 2 - Migration Factor

Factor	Current State	Future State
Strategy	Losing market share Need for growing business and enter additional markets	Need to expand their business into new markets
Systems and apps	Around 150 apps, half of them custom-developed and half standard enterprise software	Cloud-first strategy decided in order to go to SaaS Some legacy can't be moved to Cloud and should be replaced.
Markets	Local markets	Expand geographies
Innovation drive	Slow time to market	Faster time to market to compete with smaller companies

Usage	Some of the customer-facing apps very variable in demand while back office is rather stable	Rationalize IT capabilities Flexible platform for customer-facing apps
Economics	Limited investment capacity Most of the budget dedicated to maintaining current systems and apps Every five years, big investments to renew data center	Rationalize IT spending No needs of big hardware renewal investments Reduce Cloud TCO
Legacy	Two hundred-plus legacy applications	Many won't be moved to Cloud (any Cloud) for five years or more.
IT skills	Mostly for app maintenance and project management Most development is outsourced.	Transform its IT organization to manage services
Staffing	Small IT team with limited developer skills	Likely to want packaged solutions that allow them to gain rapid benefit, even with a cost premium
Well-understood usage	Applications well understood in the usage characteristics (limited short-term scale needs)	Having limited elasticity requirements means the "massive" scale of Public Cloud doesn't provide additional value.
Agility in moderation	Agility is desired for competitive advantage.	Rapid delivery is important but not measured the same way as an internet-driven business. (Days versus months is okay.)

| Steady moderate growth | Business growth of 7 percent or less CAGR | Growth implies fewer surprises for IT requirements at scale. |
| No real geo-distribution needs | Limited geographic diversity requirements of apps | Have a few locations but primary app usage is at headquarters |

Recommendation

The likely answer for scenario 2 is Private Cloud, with Public Cloud used for a few applications and some development. The fact that the majority of workloads are well understood and don't experience significant usage spikes means that a slightly overprovisioned Private Cloud environment is likely more cost effective in the long run.

The limited size and experience of the team also means they would most likely benefit from a packaged Cloud solution (converged infrastructure with a Cloud management platform). As speed isn't the primary requirement and there are only a few key office locations, the need for a widely distributed Public Cloud-based application set is reduced for customer-facing applications and systems. The focus for new applications should be on SaaS wherever possible.

3.6.6 Scenario 3: Twenty-Plus-Year-Old Large Financial Institution

Company

A twenty-plus-year-old large financial Institution is a very big company with millions in revenue. It operates globally in different critical sectors: insurance, banking, and investment. Its size and strict procedures make the company unable to make any changes in the short term. Additionally, due to its business nature, most of the data should be kept in the country because of data regulations.

Migration Factors

Table 3.4 - Scenario 3 - Migration Factors

Factor	Current State	Future State
Legacy applications	Thousands of custom-built applications, some delivering millions in revenue	Some projects to retire or move applications to stateless environments Heavy focus on building new apps for Cloud Many existing apps impossible to move to Public Cloud
Staffing	Large IT team focused on enabling large-scale, cost-effective, performance-oriented infrastructure	Solutions that scale, potentially involve staff investment in open source (e.g., OpenStack / CloudStack / RedHat / Automation, etc.)
Elasticity, geo-diversity, support structure	Extreme elasticity applies to a few key apps for trading, Monte Carlo, big data analytics, etc.	In some cases, Public Cloud/grid infrastructure could handle this. Some applications will be better suited in Hybrid/ Private Cloud.
Agility	Agility is a driver like most businesses but is not the sole reason for Cloud operations.	Agility is measured in days versus months.
Steady growth, geo-distributed, heavy IT investment	Business growth of approximately 12 percent CAGR	Growth is fairly well understood.

| Geo-distribution | Widely distributed workforce with developers and contributors in offices all over the world

Also a customer base that is globally distributed and dynamic | Geodiversity is critical for application, performance, and fault tolerance. |
|---|---|---|
| Compliance | Heavy regulatory and compliance-based risks | Require contractual guarantee with providers or internal solutions |

Recommendations

This last scenario has an environment quite complex and doesn't fit into a single solution. The fact that they have a strong IT team and large internal set of applications means Private Cloud is a real option for them. They are also likely in a position to be able to develop unique Private Cloud environments instead of focusing on prepackaged converged infrastructure.

However, Public Cloud is potentially an ideal solution for some of the customer-focused applications and/or applications requiring elasticity at scale. Public Cloud could be a very good solution for nonproduction environments to make new application deployment more agile.

An open item is compliance. Using Public Cloud would depend on the provider's credentials along with usage trends for any given application.

4 Cloud Governance

Companies and other organizations commonly have what is known as corporate governance, which is a set or collection of the processes, policies and procedures, rules, applicable laws, and regulations by which the corporation is organized, operated, administered, and controlled.

And in today's private business and public institutions, many, if not most, of the corporate governance processes are directly or indirectly supported by all types of IT systems, which require their own set of rules and processes to ensure the efficient use of the IT resources that support the business strategies and objectives. That set of rules is known as the company IT governance.

With the evolution of technology and emergence of Cloud computing and the changes it involves, it has also become necessary to define the policies and procedures for an optimal use of Cloud resources for organizations. This set of processes, policies, and procedures is known as Cloud governance. Figure 4.1 shows an overview of the governance layers.

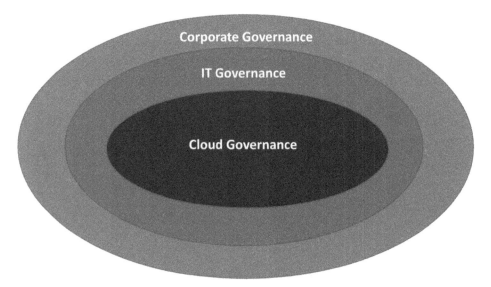

Figure 4.1 – Corporate, IT and Cloud Governance

From an overall perspective of a company or an organization, we could see that there is a general corporate governance, which includes all business processes from sales, procurement, financial, or production processes to human resources, investor relationships, and any other relevant company process. In current times, most business processes are supported by technology, which is ruled by its own IT governance, and within which we will find the new Cloud IT governance model.

There might be as many IT and Cloud governance models as businesses themselves, but as long as they provide the most efficient and cost-effective IT resources in an organized and structured way to align with business strategy and objectives, they can fit the purpose. You have to create or choose the one that best fits your organization.

Those companies that are going to be intensively using hundreds or thousands of Cloud services should be particularly concerned in defining a good model and making sure their organization is aware and trained, and changes communicated. Smaller organizations might not require a deep Cloud governance model, but the pillars should be there, as they could well grow and need additional services.

Some of the aspects of the Cloud governance model that are more tightly related with Cloud adoption and migration are explained in detail in other chapters of the book, like the CRA (chapter 5 of this first volume) or service management (chapter 4 of the second volume of this book).

In this chapter, we introduce one of the many possible Cloud IT governance models and those relevant aspects for Cloud adoption and migration that are not directly covered in other parts of the book.

4.1   IT Governance and IT Service Management (ITSM) in the Cloud Age

Cloud governance is part of the general IT governance when the company strategy is not fully Cloud-based. For those all-Cloud companies, IT governance and Cloud governance are the same; they are based and structured on a single Cloud IT governance.

For those organizations that have a sound IT governance in place, transitioning their IT service management (ITSM) should already have a good base for supporting and managing Cloud and hybrid services and environments.

The Cloud is going to change the way that IT services and resources are provided. So the challenge and key aspects is to successfully transition from traditional ITSM (only considered on-premises resources) to a Cloud-based service management, which means you need to include your Cloud governance within the general IT governance.

There are many models for implementing IT governance within companies, with IT Infrastructure Library (ITIL) one of the most common ones, but there are many other popular ones such as Control Objectives for Information and Related Technologies (COBIT).

If you have ITIL at least partially implemented, you have a good foundation for moving or adapting it to the Cloud, especially to hybrid environments. Since the main objective is to make IT more efficient and optimize the use of Cloud resources, Cloud governance for those companies coming from ITIL must adapt to the changes that comes with it, like variable costs, procurement, deployment, automation, integration options, service catalog, and demand management.

Your Cloud governance or Cloud ITSM must adapt to your Cloud strategies, which can be many: All-Cloud, Hybrid, Multi-Cloud, different type of services (IaaS, PaaS, SaaS, or serverless), networking and communications, security, and so forth. As companies evolve and progress in their Cloud journies and strategies, the complexity of managing and organizing IT also increases. But it also creates opportunities.

Governance for Cloud becomes more relevant to the organizations than it was with traditional on-premises IT in order to benefit from the agility and flexibility that Cloud services offer. Organizations need to understand and learn how to take advantage of those benefits, which requires them to have in place the processes, policies, resources, and tooling (Cloud governance) to make a proper use of their IT resources with the objective of better supporting their business processes and company strategies.

A sound governance can help organizations maximize their investments by profiting from the available and upcoming capabilities offered by the Cloud. Without proper governance, it will be quite difficult to get the expected benefits offered by the new technology.

4.2 A Cloud Governance Model for Cloud-Oriented Organizations

Cloud governance, or IT governance for a Cloud strategy and a Cloud-oriented organization, is the design and creation of a Cloud operating model: policies, principles, and processes for the correct and optimal use of Cloud computing services. The main objectives of defining and using a Cloud governance are to

- create value by optimizing the benefits of IT resources;
- align business goals with cost and investments in the Cloud;
- establish the correct degree of investment and control in the Cloud service's life cycle;
- automate tasks and advance securitization of corporate secrets; and
- ensure the security and regulatory compliance of information in the Cloud (with special attention to ISO 27001).

From the point of view of Cloud adoption and migration, the most important aspects of the Cloud governance model to consider are the following.

The CRA (Most Specifically, the Deployment View)

You should have your Cloud services structured in the best way possible from the beginning, at least from a general perspective. If you don't do it right from the beginning, changes might be costly in time and might have some other timing and cost-related consequences.

Service Management

Before any Cloud Service is set into a production state (users will perform any type of work), it is extremely important to ensure the reliability, support, administration, and incident management. Remember that even having a development system in the Cloud must be supported and protected. You don't want to waste the time and money it takes to develop.

Cost Management

The extreme facility of provisioning Cloud services can give the impression of a free smorgasbord, and if the policies are not controlled properly, you might find unexpected high costs and bills. Cloud governance should provide the procedures and mechanisms to avoid the cloud-sprawling effect. At the same time, you don't want to set up excessive administrative processes for procurement of services in the Cloud, losing the new agility that is being provided. The right balance between Cloud agility and procedures can be achieved by the use of process and service management automation.

The Cloud adoption and migration master plan is an umbrella covering most aspects of the CGM (Cloud Governance Model), but as with our pragmatic approach, we have given more focus on acknowledgement and training (since it impacts the people and organization); the CRA (basic for designing and deployments); cost management; service management; and automation.

Figure 4.2 shows one comprehensive model of Cloud governance, specifically targeting Cloud-oriented organizations.

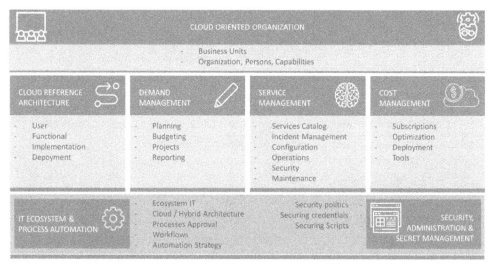

Figure 4.2 – Cloud Governance Model for
a Cloud Oriented Organization

Let's have a look at each of the elements of the model. On top of the model is the organization itself: how the company is organized into teams, business units, people, and its responsibilities and capabilities. In the Cloud Age, some organizational changes, business processes, and skills will necessarily have to change or adapt to the new ways.

Cloud adoption and migration organizational challenges as well as change management were discussed in section 1.7 of the initial chapter of this book. In summary, your organization will have to adapt its current ITSM to the Cloud governance model so the business units and teams can be either trained, reskilled, or assigned to new roles. Several business processes will have to change. Look at it from a positive evolving perspective though.

In the model below the Cloud organization, you find four main areas, which are all intimately related and must function seamlessly together for proper governance:

- The CRA is the main tool or document that provides the model for discussing the requirements, structures, and operations of Cloud computing. The ISO defined the standard ISO/IEC 17789:2014 that specifies the Cloud Computing Reference Architecture (CCRA) as the reference architecture includes the Cloud computing roles, Cloud computing activities, and Cloud functional components and their relationship.
- Demand management is the set of processes by which IT departments provide the solutions to the business, matching the demand to the supply, and includes processes such as the project portfolio management, planning, and budgeting.
- Service management refers to the most operational IT tasks that need to be organized and in place in order to provide the right IT and Cloud support to the business. This includes the catalog of services, the ticketing or incident management process, configuration management, systems and application operations, maintenance tasks, and proper security services.
- Cost management provides a cost-efficient processes to provide the Cloud services to the business. Cost management is intimately related to optimizing how the business units are contracting, providing, and consuming the resources.

And underlying all of them, we also include in the model two important elements that can provide both the right balance between the overhead that might be generated by too much procedure and policy bureaucracy and agility provided by the Cloud, as well as the pillar of ensuring that the business information is protected and secure when the organization systems and applications are running in the Cloud.

- **IT ecosystem and process automation.** This refers to the processes of optimizing and organizing the IT tasks and activities required to run the business systems in the Cloud, from procuring external personnel or system integrators (IT ecosystem) to the process of optimizing workloads and resources to the automation strategy to benefit from the flexibility of the Cloud resources.
- **Security management.** This refers to the overall security strategy and policies of the organization to ensure the company information assets, the right access controls, and all the procedures and tooling that will be required to protect the company from internal and external security threats.

The next sections discuss in more detail some of the above aspects. For those that are more relevant for Cloud adoption and migration, such as the CRA (deployment view), security and service management are extensively covered in their own chapters.

4.3 People in Cloud-Oriented Organizations

For some time, especially in the early days of Cloud computing adoption, professionals within companies, in particular those within the IT departments, were afraid of losing their jobs because of moving systems to the Cloud, and this often provoked an initial rejection to the Cloud computing service models. Currently this feeling has greatly diminished, but it is still quite important to consider the changing roles for the company's internal professionals in order to properly transition to the Cloud.

4.3.1   What Changes in IT Departments with Cloud Computing

In the beginning, Cloud computing needs individuals with strong managerial skills because they must be able to take the initiative to evaluate all that Cloud computing has to offer. Once those individuals recognize that Cloud is not killing IT, but simply redefining it, the time to move forward will have arrived.

The company should then move forward with creating its strategy relating to how it will move to the Cloud. This will include how the company will handle negotiating services, how they will handle contracts related to Cloud providers, and what the role of the company's procurement department and legal firm will look like as the company moves toward the Cloud. There will also be the need to choose Cloud services and applications that are appropriate for the company and aligned with its business strategy.

As more and more companies take their businesses to the Cloud, the need for a number of different Cloud professionals is going to continue to grow. There will be a demand for many different Cloud professionals, such as Cloud network engineers, Cloud product managers, Cloud consultants, Cloud systems engineers, Cloud developers, Cloud system administrators, Cloud sales executives, Cloud software engineers, and Cloud engineers.

Innovation and vision skills will definitely be necessary for Cloud jobs. In addition, Cloud jobs will require skills in leadership, business communication, project management, planning, architectural skills, analysis, supplier relations, negotiations, and technical proficiency, to name just a few of the skill areas that are going to be in great need.

Cloud computing offers a new way of doing business, a fresh take, so to speak. It is very important that Cloud computing professionals understand how to maximize the use of Cloud computing so they can run the entire enterprise.

The best way to know if a Cloud service will meet your company's needs is to set up a simulation. Doing this will allow you the opportunity to run your business needs through the Cloud service to ensure it is living up to the expectations.

Another important Cloud computing skill is leadership. Cloud applications need to be brought into the company with a goal to improve the overall business performance, and so there is a need for strong leadership skills to implement the Cloud applications.

Cloud computing professionals need to negotiate with Cloud vendors, always keeping what is best for the company in mind. Cloud professionals need to have the skills to ask the necessary questions about physical location, SLAs, data availability, service interruptions, and intellectual property rights.

The planning stage is important, and Cloud computing professionals are also expected to create a Cloud implementation roadmap for the company. Finally cloud computing professionals need to have technical proficiency so they secure business operations in the Cloud in the manner that will work best for the business and offer the most viability.

Even though some believe the Cloud is killing IT, this is simply not true. The Cloud is redefining IT, offering several interesting career opportunities.

4.3.2   Cloud Computing Skills for IT Departments

As Cloud adoption and migrations are taking over and whether you will be managing it yourself or in the cases where your company might be using an external managed Cloud service provider, skills in IT and job descriptions will change when adopting a Cloud model.

The objectives of IT can be aligned with business strategies more than ever; therefore it becomes much more important than troubleshooting and fixing IT problems, installing or replacing hardware, doing updates, or using IT to search for creating value with new business solutions.

Depending on the specific reach of your Cloud strategy, companies will have the need to have skills in their IT departments for

- Cloud strategists with a broad, innovative vision of how to better leverage and align the Cloud to the business requirements and solid knowledge on selecting the right applications and resources for the company. They are able to understand Cloud economics and evaluate the vendor offerings and contracting options.
- Cloud architects with a sound technical background. They are able to define the CRA and design required architectures for the systems and services to be deployed on the Cloud.

- Cloud service planners and project managers with planning, analysis, technical, negotiating, and designing skills. They are typically in charge of engaging the organization into the projects around new Cloud services to be implemented.
- New application and integration architects for Cloud and DevOps. These roles take care of organizing the software development process to ensure effective application development and delivery according to business requirements
- Network engineers, in charge of designing, deploying and managing network topology and communications elements, to ensure connectivity among applications, systems and users.
- Security experts. They have the responsibility of defining the security policies and ensuring that your assets in the Cloud are protected against unauthorized users or external threads.
- Cloud and subscription system admins with the necessary technical proficiency in order to secure the operations of the business in the Cloud
- Cloud software engineers. These roles are becoming increasingly important due to the fact that there are so many possibilities for software and application design and development. They are typically in charge of looking for the best possible solutions that fits the business requirements.
- Leadership needed to bring those Cloud benefits into new applications to improve the business. This includes negotiating Cloud contracts with Cloud vendors: IP rights, regions and locations, availability, security, compliance and certifications, SLAs, maintenance windows, and so on.

4.4 Introduction to the Cloud Reference Architecture (CRA)

A CRA provides a methodological framework for a model or reference for organizations that adopt or migrate to the Cloud. This framework defines the architectural components, the policies and procedures, and the roles and responsibilities of stakeholders for the right Cloud services deployment, service management, orchestration, and security.

The next chapter in this book introduces the CRA as defined in "ISO/IEC 17789 Cloud Computing Architecture" with great focus and practical examples (based on Microsoft Azure) on the deployment view. Having a reference architecture when migrating workloads to the Cloud helps you ensure security, manageability, compliance, and consistency when deploying Cloud-based resources.

We strongly recommend having at least a basic version of the deployment view of a CRA before any deployment takes place in your Cloud subscription. If you fail to do so, you take the risk of having to modify many of the Cloud resource attributes later on, which might result in unnecessary redeployments and downtimes.

Without at least a basic CRA you might end up with a Cloud architecture and infrastructure that is more difficult to understand, manage, and support. Having a nonstructured Cloud setup and architecture with the right naming conventions, security design, or networking can lead to additional costs, and even the violation of security and compliance policies in the enterprise in some cases. Systems and applications could end up deployed in an unmanageable way, in different silos with difficult connectivity and security or access management holes, which might open doors to potential threats.

These are the reasons why we included the definition of the CRA as the fifth phase in the preparation stage of the migration master plan.

4.5   IT Demand Management in Cloud

In standard terminology, demand management is a planning methodology used to forecast, plan for, and manage the demand for products and services. This can be at macrolevels as in economics and at microlevels within individual organizations.

In regards to IT and according to ITIL methodology, the purpose of demand management is to understand, anticipate, and influence customer demand for services. As a process, it is part of the ITIL service strategy stage of the ITIL life cycle. Service strategy determines which services to offer to prospective customers or markets.

Failure to define a clear demand management for the Cloud services and resources to match the needs of the organizations and its business units, with the rules, responsibilities, and policies, can compromise the objectives of Cloud sourcing. IT sourcing executives who collaborate with IT executives to develop IT demand discipline will successfully prioritize and optimize the utilization of Cloud services.

Since Cloud governance sets the procedures and policies to provide optimal use of Cloud resources to the organizations, there is a need to meet business demands with proper demand management processes. In this sense, demand management for the Cloud is quite similar to the processes of more traditional sourcing of on-premises IT resources. The main processes within Cloud demand management include:

- Planning for the upcoming demand of systems, applications, and services that will use Cloud resources to meet enterprise requirements for technology. Considerations in Cloud governance have to do with the fact that procurement and provision can be quite accelerated, so lead times are considerably shorter. Dependencies between projects and requests are one of the most important aspects to consider when defining a proper planning.
- Budgeting, one of the main differences between on-premises models and the Cloud. With the switch from fixed costs to variable costs and from CAPEX to OPEX, this will require changing some of the usual financial business processes regarding budgeting. Here a common practice is to establish hard and soft limits for spending when it comes to consuming Cloud resources.
- Project management to control the planning, human and IT resources, and activities of the business requests for implementing the required solutions.
- Reporting for providing the metrics and KPIs of the demands being received in order to control the overall achievements of the business requests.

In general, demand management is very similar in the Cloud in how it's done traditionally with added agility, changing the budgeting process and considering that time to market and time to value are significantly reduced.

4.6   Cloud Service Management

Cloud service management includes all processes, policies, and controls that are needed to provide the right support and services to the business to optimize the Cloud resources and make sure the investments in Cloud are providing the expected benefits and agility. These processes include all the activities required to design, operate, control, deliver, and support the Cloud resources and services that enterprises and organizations are consuming.

Similar to ITSM in traditional on-premises models, there is a parallel correspondence with the areas included within Cloud service management.

- Cloud service catalog contains a comprehensive list of services (IT-related only) that the organization will provide to its business users and/or its business partners (including customers) using Cloud resources.
- Service request management includes the processes, policies, and procedures with which end business users interact and make requests to IT for soliciting any of the services from the Cloud service catalog. It usually requires the use of tools and definition of processes and policies to be documented and communicated.
- Incident management is the process by which the service provider tracks, measures, troubleshoots, and solves events that might affect the ability of the provided services to effectively support their IT needs. It requires ticketing tool, processes, and policies to be documented and communicated. It should contain the processes for engaging and communicating between customer and service providers, along with escalation processes and SLAs.
- Configuration management database records the configuration of all the IT systems and Cloud services and the resources being maintained. It is used also to map the business services to the provided systems and applications.
- Cloud security management is the process by which the service provider develops, implements, and supports the policies and procedures of the IT assets, in this case, only at the logical level.

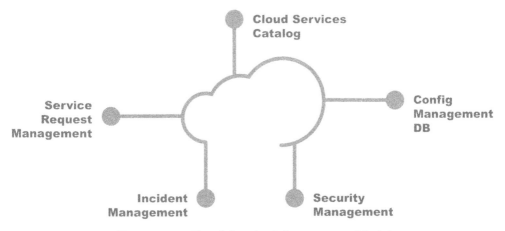

Figure 4.3 – Cloud Service Management Model

Cloud service management is a critical aspect of the Cloud migration master plan, as well as when starting the Cloud adoption, and for that reason, we have included a full chapter in the second volume of this book.

4.7   Cloud Cost Management

Managing costs in the Cloud becomes a very critical process to efficiently control the consumption, use, and costs of your resources and assets in the Cloud. The Cloud's elasticity and scalability brings with it a very elastic billing tag.

Cost control and associated budgeting are topics that are more complex on the Cloud than on traditional on-premises computing. For this reason, the main Public Cloud vendors usually offer a lot of tooling and software for Cloud cost management, and third-party software companies have developed many to help organizations control their spending on Cloud services and resources and optimize them.

To realize the Cloud benefits, enterprises need to ensure that their spending on Cloud resources will not undermine their strategy. As we introduced previously, comparing only direct costs is not always the right metric or measure to make a decision on whether the Cloud is providing expected benefits or, on the contrary, becoming a higher cost than traditional computing.

An issue that is increasingly worrying Cloud-oriented organizations has to do with finding the right balance between the agility provided and the associated cost, more specifically, trying to avoid the impression to business units that the Cloud is an infinite and free buffet of IT resources, which leads to the feared Cloud sprawling: the proliferation of uncontrolled Cloud instances and services within an organization, which happens when enterprises do not have a right Cloud governance in place.

Main Cloud vendors provide several mechanisms to avoid some of the issues associated with Cloud sprawling and cost control, such as quotas, billing monitoring, capability to set spending limits, and authorization and access controls. But often this is not enough, especially for optimizing costs and resources so companies don't overspend and are caught in insufficient capacity or budgeting for their technology needs.

For these reasons, there is an increased need for monitoring and controlling the usage and consumption of Cloud services. Cloud-oriented enterprises need efficient cost management processes so they can have visibility, monitoring, control, accountability, and predictive intelligence to align the company's strategies with the Cloud assets.

Each Cloud type and Cloud vendor can have different pricing for the resources they offer. The Cloud offerings and service types are increasing at a very rapid pace, and so are the ways of billing them. Often the problem with cost management is that it is not always easy or clear how these services are really measured and billed. And what are the differences between them? You might find some differences among different Cloud vendors have to do with:

- Billing methods. In pay-as-you-go model, pricing can be measured by the second, minute, hour, day, or month. While monthly billing is more typical in SaaS offerings. Public Cloud vendors usually offer IaaS or PaaS by the second or minute.
- Base or setup fee (if any), what it includes, and what the additional charges can be
- Discounts on consumption volume and type of resources
- Minimum commitments on consumption (if any)
- SLAs, including committed uptime and what you get back if there is a breach of the committed SLA
- The support and maintenance services included

- Business continuity options included within pricing (if any), like disaster recovery or high availability, or how much extra you have to set up and pay (if applicable)
- Tooling for proactively monitoring your Cloud resources and allowing to run administration and support operations
- The degree of their share responsibility model being actually performed. Will your Cloud vendor guarantee the performance and update of your platform when consuming PaaS?
- Networking, communication, and data transfer fees can highly vary among vendors.

Cloud cost management can provide the right processes and policies to make a better, more economic, and more efficient use of your Cloud assets and ensure the right balance between costs and capacity. There are many possibilities for optimization (which we deal with in deeper detail with practical examples in chapter 5 of the second volume), but just to mention a few:

- Selecting the right billing model. For example between pay per use or reserved instances. While pay per use is usually recommended for systems that do not need to be running permanently (like development or test systems, demo, training, archived servers, etc.), using reserved instances is usually a better option for productive systems.
- Cloud scalability makes it easy and quick to right-size your resources to actual needs. This can be a question of both sizing and correctly designing your Cloud architecture.
- Snoozing your Cloud resources: setting up a schedule for starting and stopping resources that do not need to be up and running 24/7.
- Transferring your current operating system or platform licensing can significantly lower your costs if your Cloud vendor allows for it.
- Automating the process of demand and provisioning with an associated budget and with the right access and approval controls
- Negotiating your Cloud contracts and understanding what you are getting for your bucks

In summary, efficient Cloud cost management needs to be put in place as part of the Cloud governance model for the following reasons:

- Allocate your budges and predicted costs for an effective control and use of your Cloud resources
- Avoid Cloud sprawling
- Set up alerts and thresholds for spending and avoiding overruns
- Be able to predict costs and adjust budgets
- Have the capacity for scaling, right-sizing, and optimizing your resources
- Control the access to the Cloud resources without losing agility
- Detect any anomalies in the use and consumption

As Cloud becomes the new normal in your enterprise IT needs and your organization evolves into the innovation phase on your enterprise journey to Cloud, you will realize the many options for controlling costs and optimizing them. In the following sections, we are providing an extensive checklist of how to negotiate your contracts with Cloud providers.

4.8   Negotiating Cloud Contracts

Cloud computing is great, and one of the reasons that CFOs and CEOs are choosing this way of consuming IT resources is that it allows to reduce capital expenses and costs while increasing speed, flexibility, time to value, business agility, and capacity for innovation. Still Cloud comes with regular invoicing and a price tag, one that often can be much more complicated than what it might seem at first sight.

Maintaining a good relationship between customers and vendors during the life of a contract is good for both and something everybody should aim for. A good customer/vendor relationship is going to be based on setting the right expectations about the services and the costs. Vendors providing great service at a great cost value will have happy customers who most likely will remain loyal. However, customers finding that their Cloud vendors are either underperforming in their services or charging hidden or unexpected fees will most likely first complain and then cancel the contract and switch to a different vendor.

Of course, it's not always easy or cheap to switch vendors, and the issue of the degree of your Cloud vendor lock-in must be considered in your Cloud strategy. It is essential to be well informed and to know exactly what you are contracting and what costs, fees, and services you should be expecting.

Whether you might be contracting any type of IaaS, PaaS, SaaS, and its many variants and subtypes, each Cloud vendor might charge quite differently, and the number of options might be quite large and sometimes complicated to understand.

There are many topics to discuss with your Cloud vendor(s), and often you might be using more than one in a multi-Cloud strategy (e.g., having IaaS/PaaS on one Cloud provider and one or several SaaS applications with other vendors).

In the sections below, we're summarizing ten issues to consider, which we think are the most important ones for most customers. These topics are all related with each other.

4.8.1   Fees, Pricing, and Invoicing

The first issue is to know what, when, and how you will be charged with. A practical approach is to define the baseline services you are getting, like number or type of VMs, storage, applications, platforms, number, types of users, and so on. Once the baseline is established, make sure you understand whether you will be charged or not for extras. (This is very dependent on the type of Cloud service.)

- Extra storage needs (especially in PaaS or SaaS). While it's typically charged in IaaS contracts, some SaaS vendors offer unlimited storage.
- On-demand pricing. How much will you be charged when your servers and applications are not running? For example, when using VMs, you are not charged for them when you stop them, but you will be charged for the disk or storage space of the images of the VMs.
- Will you get fixed fees and prices, or can they change over the life of the contract?
- Do you have to pay for mobile access (especially in SaaS)?

- Which add-ons or additional Cloud services will be charged in case of activation and deployment?
- Are there discounts based on volume contract, consumption, or contract duration?
- What happens with the fees when we need more/less resources or users to be added/subtracted from the contract? (Sometimes scalability in contracts works well for adding up, but not so well for decreasing number of users, especially in SaaS contracts.)
- Will you be charged for integrating your Cloud service with on-premises systems or applications (*hybrid landscapes*)? For example, Public Cloud vendors typically charge for the egress traffic (downloading data or data coming out of the Cloud).
- Will we be charged if we need to make an extra system copy for testing (typical in SaaS environments)?
- Is disaster recovery included in the fees?

There might be other charges associated with some of the topics we discuss below.

4.8.2   *Ending and Cancelling the Contract*

This is an important aspect for your legal department to carefully review. Pay attention carefully to the following:

- How and when can the contract be cancelled? In SaaS, this might be a tricky issue, while in IaaS/PaaS, in general, it is easier, unless you have contracted reserved instances for one or three years, in which case, you might need to pay a cancellation fee or penalty.
- Are there any penalties for early cancellation? And if so, explain well.
- Is there automatic renewal? If so, will the same terms apply?
- What will happen with your systems/data/information should the contract be cancelled (important in SaaS systems)? If you are changing providers, a migration project should be considered.
- Are there different options to recover your data should you want to migrate to another system or vendor?
- Will you get a refund if you paid services in advance?

4.8.3 Services Setup and Deployment Costs

Make sure you understand if there are any fees or charges for setting up the Cloud services you are contracting. Of course, for the most comprehensive applications offered in SaaS mode, there will be costs associated with configuring and implementing the system, but that might be contracted with a specific professional service provider.

In case of setting up IaaS/PaaS, there is also cost associated with configuring the architecture, services, and security for your landing zones in the Cloud, but it's completely your responsibility, except for those tasks that fall under the umbrella of the vendor's responsibility.

4.8.4 Maintenance, Operations, and Support

One of the economic reasons for choosing and moving to Cloud is to actually hand over routine maintenance and operations to your Cloud vendor and/or your Cloud managed service provider depending on the delivery models chosen, such as performing backups/restores; installing upgrades, fixes, or upgrades; or monitoring the state of the systems, the platform, the applications, and the like. And all of them will offer you some type and degree of support.

Again the delivery model will significantly impact the covered services. While SaaS providers will typically take care of upgrading every tenant to the next release and sending the customers a new upgraded tenant for testing, upgrading is not common in IaaS models, except for the underlying hardware, which you will typically not even notice. In PaaS models, there are managed services included up to the middleware or platform layer. Some of the factors you need to understand from your vendor are the following:

- Which maintenance services are included in the contract?
- Are backup/restore operations included? How many? What is the backup policy? Can we select other backup policies/periods?
- What type of system/application monitoring do you do?
- How do we contact support? What is the availability of the support?
- Is minor/major upgrading included?

- Does your maintenance include system copies of our SaaS tenants?
- Do we have the possibility of a snapshot copy before a critical test/operation and to restore it in case something goes wrong?
- What other value-added services are included in our contract?
- Is the support provided in different languages/time zones?

4.8.5 *Security and Business Continuity*

Unless you are part of a very large corporation with deep pockets for investing in security, most certain is that your Cloud provider should provide very high security standards and certifications, but nevertheless, this is one critical issue that requires very good understanding and expectations by customers since it's also one of the main reasons and objections for opposing Cloud adoption.

You should request a document or presentation by your Cloud provider that explains their security policies, certifications, and standards in their Cloud data centers. If your company belongs to an industry sector that requires additional measures concerning the access and privacy of the information held in the systems, such as HIPAA for the health industry, your Cloud vendor should inform if they include this type of compliance and security standard.

If there is a CSO in your organization, she or he will have many questions for the Cloud provider. Here we just include a few of what we consider the most important ones:

- Which security certifications do they have, and what are each of them for?
- What types of data encryption process is used from the customer to the Cloud services.
- How are my systems/data safeguarded from other customers or government agencies?
- In case of a failure in the data center where our systems/applications/data is located, is there any business continuity procedure in place, such as automatic failover or disaster recovery?
- How do you destroy our systems and information after we cancel the contract?

- What happens in case of data corruption?
- How long does it take for a restore copy to be applied?

4.8.6 *Localization and Compliance*

Closely related with security are the issues you need to understand regarding localization and compliance. In the case of compliance, it might have legal implications and regulations that often are not well known by IT departments, so it's a good practice to consult about it or really ask your Cloud vendor about it.

- In which country/countries are our systems physically located?
- In case of a SaaS application, is it localized for the country/countries where we operate?
- Are your systems compliant with the laws and regulations required by our country/countries and the industry where we do business in?

4.8.7 Performance

Performance involves your Cloud provider but also your networking capabilities, bandwidth, and configuration. Actually network latency and bandwidth is one of the critical reasons for the success of a transition to the Cloud; otherwise you might be placing your company users at risk of not using and not accepting the new systems due to excessive response times.

This is probably the one issue where on-premises systems are still a bit ahead of the Cloud counterpart; therefore it is of critical importance. Obviously it's also one of the topics that Cloud vendors and providers are working harder at, and we should soon see great improvements.

Depending on the Cloud service type, performance can be measured differently. In case of SaaS systems and applications, it could be established as the average **response time** that users get when executing application transactions either online or in batch. You should analyze with your provider the average response time considering elements involved: CPU, database response time, networking time, and maybe others.

Your IT must hold deep and technical conversations with your

Cloud vendors, especially in those cases where there are mission-critical applications and systems involved. Set your performance expectations right, and get your networking assessed, improved, and updated. Then make sure you have alternative ways and failover procedures for accessing your systems in the Cloud should your primary networking backbone fail.

There is also another topic regarding performance by your Cloud provider: **provisioning time**. This should be n times faster than when provisioning for on-site on-premises systems; however, it's a very recommended practice to have the right expectations and knowing how long it takes to provision different types of Cloud services such as VM, storage, web platforms, and, most importantly, SaaS. This is important because if you decide to implement advanced ways of resource elasticity, it might become an issue with a considerable cost element in large Cloud landscapes.

4.8.8 Service Level Agreements (SLAs)

SLAs are the base of your contract with your Cloud service provider and the guarantee of getting a good service, so pay particular attention to them since the commitment of your provider with the SLAs offered is critical to your systems and applications availability, scalability, and performance. Additionally SLAs might have contractual obligations by the vendor, and some even guarantee refunding part of the fees if the SLAs are not met. Some of the most common SLAs you should be looking at include:

- systems and applications availability (monthly, yearly)
- maintenance windows schedule
- provisioning time of different computing services
- support response times according to ticket priorities
- response times
- business continuity and/or disaster recovery times (When is it triggered? How long from failure to failover availability?)
- times for customer-requested operations (e.g., restore, snapshots, systems copy, updates, etc.)

4.8.9   *Scalability and Elasticity*

Scalability and elasticity are two of the basic characteristics that Cloud computing must provide; however, one must look closely at both and how they will affect your fees. We have mentioned them in the first issue. But to get expectations right and avoid charging surprises, ask your Cloud vendor questions such as:

- Can we set up automatic scalability based on certain parameters (typically average CPU usage, response times, number of requests, etc.)?
- How can we control self-service for adding up or subtracting Cloud resources?
- How much will it cost to have dormant resources to be used only in peak periods?
- If you contract a type of computing resource, how will it affect the fees if for whatever reason our company needs much less computing power or application users? Will that be possible in the contract?
- If we increase the number of users in a PaaS or SaaS application, will we get the same SLAs?

Automatic elasticity is only partially available in some services, typically in IaaS types, and often must be manually programmed by customers using scripts. It's one of those Cloud issues that has yet to be enhanced to be as fully automated as businesses would like. Have your Cloud vendor tell you all about their features and options concerning up-and-down scalability and how much automated it is.

4.8.10   *Monitoring and Reporting*

The last issue you should pay attention to is the type, depth, and autonomy you will have for monitoring your usage, consumption, and Cloud resources and the reporting that your Cloud vendor will provide, whether it will be built-in or sent to you periodically.

In order to contrast that you are being charged correctly and ensure you have a correct governance, you need to have access to detailed reporting on:

- **Usage** of Cloud computing resources, types, number of users, and any other type of Cloud service you might have deployed
- **SLAs and availability** (also a good practice to request reports on schedule maintenance)
- **Access log** (might be required for compliance or as part of your security policy)
- **Performance**
- **Billing and invoicing**
- **Security report** (whether there have been security incidents, attacks, or any other issues)

Your vendor might provide reporting in a self-service fashion. It might be obtained through advance tooling or sent to you periodically by your Cloud vendor or managed Cloud service provider. Sometimes due to complex landscapes, you might need to deploy some type of Cloud service management tools to have a deep overview of your environments.

There are other issues when negotiating with your Cloud provider, such as training, service catalog, monitoring tools, inter-Cloud integration costs, and so on, but we think the ten issues we have described above will cover most of your requirements.

4.9   IT Process Automation

Another important element within a comprehensive Cloud governance model has to do with the capability to orchestrate and integrate the processes, tooling, and people through a sequence of coordinated activities (workflows), mostly through automation, although some manual decisions are activities that still must be performed. This is what is known as IT process automation. That gets a lot of relevance in the Cloud due to the implicit capabilities that Cloud computing provides.

In a way, IT process automation (ITPA) is the glue that sticks together all the governance elements and provides a way of improving the overall governance activities, either replacing or improving human tasks, making a much more efficient control and use of the Cloud resources, and providing a much better integration among processes and systems. Benefits brought by ITPA includes the following:

- Having the IT processes documented, modeled, and optimized
- Better and more efficient control of the IT activities
- Faster response to requests, demands, and support issues
- Reduced errors and risks
- Standardization of processes and operations
- Better meeting of security and compliance requirements within processes and activities
- Management and control of allocation of resources and therefore cost management
- Ability to include the organization ecosystem with the IT processes

Cloud computing capabilities provide unprecedented advantages for automation since Public Cloud makes immediately available and ready to use all types and flavors of Cloud services, making it much easier and faster to design and deploy them.

In the specific case of the deployment view of the CRA, automation provides the ability of having a repository of ready-to-use automated scripts or templates for quick and repeated deployment (infrastructure as code). This improves the capability of reusing the same components for different processes and activities, which are easier to maintain, scale, and replicate.

Chapter 5 of the second volume of this book provides a very detailed description and lots of real examples on automation in general and automation in the Cloud in particular.

4.10   Cloud Security Management

Managing security in the Cloud is another part of the components and processes of the Cloud governance model, which is key to protect the enterprise's and organization's information assets and is critical to business.

Security has been—and still is—one of the topics more sensitive to the enterprises when taking their journey to Cloud since there is the perception—in part, in reality—of losing control on how your data is being controlled and managed and who could access it. Assuring security and privacy practices and procedures can overcome the challenges and objections to Cloud and will attract more enterprises to Cloud computing strategies and models.

Cloud security refers to a broad set of policies, technologies, applications, and controls utilized to protect virtualized IP, data, applications, services, and associated infrastructure of Cloud computing resources.

Managing the Cloud security is extremely important for every aspect of the Cloud adoption and migration master plan and directly or indirectly is a basic part of every stage and phase of it. For this reason, chapter 6 deals extensively with the topic of managing security in the Cloud.

5 Cloud Reference Architecture

This chapter introduces the Cloud Reference Architecture (CRA) as defined in "ISO/IEC 17789 Cloud Computing Architecture" with great focus on the deployment view. Having a reference architecture when migrating workloads to the Cloud helps you ensure security, manageability, compliance, and consistency when deploying Cloud-based resources.

You will learn the building blocks of Cloud migration from deployment perspective, which starts with defining an enterprise structure or scaffold and understanding how to plan your deployment with cost and manageability in mind. You will quickly realize that there is a lot to do before even deploying the first Cloud resource. Remember always that a good planning in the beginning can save you a lot of overhead and trouble later.

As things are better explained by an example, we will go through building the CRA for an organization called myCloudCo. And since deployment details depend on the Cloud provider, we will use Microsoft Azure as the target for migrating resources. Nevertheless, the same concepts work when migrating to other Cloud providers.

We hope after reading this chapter that you realize that the goal for a successful Cloud migration project from deployment perspective is to maintain the balance between agility and governance. When you deploy applications in the Cloud, you want your developers to be empowered to provision resources and take advantage of the Cloud's automation and agility. On the other hand, you don't want to compromise security or overlook compliance and governance. This is what the CRA is trying to achieve. Let's start!

5.1   CRA Deployment View

Before digging into the definition of CRA and its benefits, it is better to look at how things can go wrong without having one. You will quickly realize that it is better to spend some time before migration to understand and plan your Cloud deployment. Doing that will not only save you time and money, but will help you meet your security and governance needs.

5.1.1   Explaining the Need for CRA

When organizations start planning their Cloud migration, like anything else new, they start by trying and testing some capabilities. Perhaps they start to host their development environment in the Cloud while keeping their production one on premises.

It is also common to see small and perhaps isolated applications being migrated first, perhaps because of their size and low criticality, and to give the Cloud a chance to prove it is trustworthy. After all, migration to the Cloud is a journey and doesn't happen overnight.

Then the benefits of Cloud solutions become apparent, and companies start to migrate multiple large-scale workloads. As more and more workloads move to the Cloud, many organizations find themselves dealing with workload islands that are managed separately with different security models and independent data flows. Even worse, with the pressure to get new applications deployed in the Cloud with strict deadlines, developers find themselves rushing to consume new services without reasonable consideration to the organization's security and governance needs.

The unfortunate result in most cases is to end up with a Cloud infrastructure that is hard to manage and maintain. Each application could end up deployed on a separate island with its own connectivity infrastructure and with poor access management.

Furthermore, managing costs of running workloads in the Cloud becomes a challenge. The lack of automation, naming conventions, and security models are hard to achieve afterward. Even worse, data can be hosted in geographies that violate corporate's compliance needs, which is a big concern for most organizations.

In **figure 5.1**, you can see different applications deployed in their own virtual networks. Each application maintains a separate security and connectivity infrastructure, which could easily lead to implementing an application with missing security equipment.

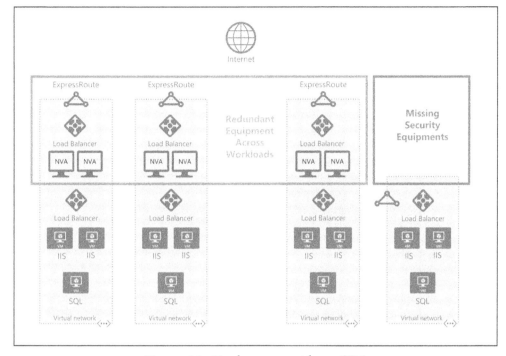

Figure 5.1 - Deployment without CRA

5.1.2 Defining CRA

Now that you understand what might go wrong without a reference architecture, let us introduce it and see how it can help you in your Cloud migration. Simply put, the CRA helps organizations address the need for detailed, modular, and current architecture guidance for building solutions in the Cloud. It serves as a collection of design guidance and design patterns to support structured approach to deploy services and applications in the Cloud.

The ISO/IEC 17789 Cloud Computing Reference Architecture defines four different views for the CRA as shown in figure 5.2: user view, fictional view, implementation view, and deployment view.

In this chapter, we address the deployment view of the CRA. The deployment view provides a framework to be used for all Cloud deployment projects, which reduces the effort during design and provides an up-front guidance for a deployment aligned to architecture, security, and compliance.

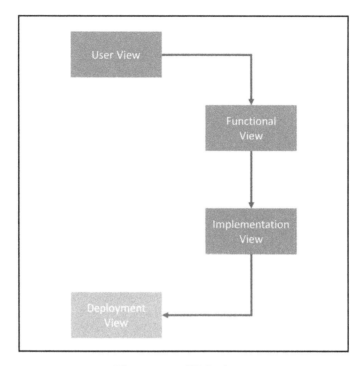

Figure 5.2 - CRA views

You can think of the deployment view of the CRA as the blueprint for all Cloud projects. The goal of this view is to help you quickly develop and implement Cloud-based solutions while reducing complexity and risk.

Therefore, having a foundation architecture helps you ensure security, manageability, compliance, and consistency for deploying resources. It includes network, security, management infrastructure, naming conventions, hybrid connectivity, and more.

Since not all organizations are the same, the deployment view does not outline a single design that fits all sizes. Rather it provides a framework for decisions based on core Cloud services, features, and capabilities.

5.1.3   Who Should Consider CRA?

You might be wondering if this applies to your case or not. Any organization that has decided to deploy resources in the Cloud can benefit from the efficiency of the CRA. Even if you have a single application, you can benefit from using the patterns and components used to establish a proper CRA.

Different teams are involved here. From one side, centralized IT, security, and compliance teams can help with enforcing policies, segregating duties, and ensuring uniformity of the underlying common components. From the other side, DevOps teams can be given more freedom and control over their environments to quickly deploy workloads without compromising security.

When planning your CRA, keep in mind that you should prefer long-term benefits over short-term benefits. Having a foundation infrastructure up front can be a lot of work to do and time-consuming. However, the long-term benefits are worth investing in.

5.1.4   Assumptions

To better understand the key concepts of the CRA, we will be defining a CRA for a sample organization and see what the process looks like. Let us assume there is an organization called myCloudCo that is planning to host its workloads on Microsoft Azure as part of a big Cloud migration project.

myCloudCo wants to lift-and-shift their main three applications to Azure, and they are working on establishing a proper CRA up front. They have a need that the computing environment hosted in Azure should consist of resources from all stages of the solution life cycle (production, dev, and QA environments).

Part of their design is to extend their on-premises network to Azure, and they are considering using ExpressRoute as the main connectivity approach, with a failover site-to-site VPN to Azure.

All VMs deployed in the Cloud should be domain-joined to their on-premises Active Directory to enforce the already configured group policies they are using for their on-premises machines. The design should also allow business units to deploy individual workloads with agility and flexibility while adhering to central IT policies. The three main applications they are migrating to the Cloud are the following:

- Corporate financial system, which the finance department manages.

- HR payroll system, which HR manages.
- Internet-facing portal, which the marketing department manages.

During the migration project, different teams play distinct, important roles and should be identified early in the process. Users are assigned to groups; groups are assigned to roles. This way it is easy to add or remove users from and to roles by adding or removing them from the corresponding groups. Table 10 list the different teams and their roles.

Group	Role	Responsibilities
Security Team	SecOps	Manages the overall security such as firewall rules and encryption.
Networking Team	NetOps	Manages network operations such as VNET, peering, and gateways.
Operations Team	SysOps	Manages computer and storage resources such as VMs and backup.
DevOps Team	DevOps	Builds workload features and applications.

Table 5.1 - Teams Involved in Cloud Migration

5.2   Defining an Enterprise Scaffold

After you decide to migrate to the Cloud and take advantage of all what the Cloud has to offer, there are a couple of concerns (shown in figure 5.3) that should be addressed first:

- Establish a governance framework to address key issues like data sovereignty.
- Develop a way to manage and track cost effectively (how you can know what resources are deployed so you can account for it and bill it back accurately).
- Deploy with mind-set of security first (defining clear management roles, access management, and security controls across all deployments).
- Building trust in the Cloud (having peace of mind that Cloud resources are managed and protected from day one).

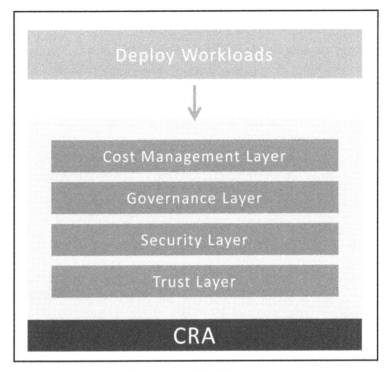

Figure 5.3 - CRA Layers

To address all these key concerns, you need to think of adopting a framework or an enterprise scaffold that can help you move to the Cloud with confidence. Think about how engineers build a structure. They start by creating the basis of the structure (scaffold) that provides anchor points for more permanent systems to be mounted.

The same applies when deploying workloads in the Cloud. You need an enterprise scaffold that provides structure to the Cloud environment and anchors for services built on top. It is the foundation that builders (IT teams) use to build services with speed of delivery in mind. The enterprise scaffold ensures that workloads you deploy in the Cloud meet the minimum security and governance practices your organization is adopting while giving developers the ability to deploy services and applications quickly to meet their goals and deadlines.

Figure 5.4 shows the components of an enterprise scaffold. The foundation relies on defining an enterprise structure and deployment essentials that you should address first. On top of that comes the need to address identity and access management and build the core networking infrastructure where services can be deployed. Resource governance and security are addressed next for all deployed resources. Furthermore, business continuity, monitoring, alerting, and logging infrastructure are common areas for all the infrastructure you build in the Cloud.

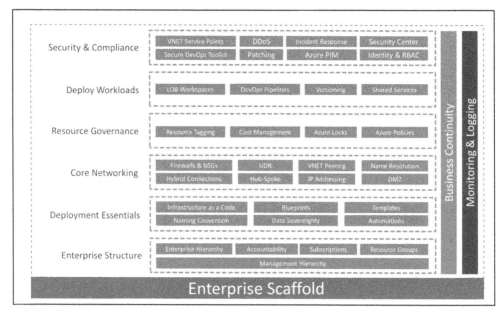

Figure 5.4 - Enterprise Scaffold

In the next sections of this chapter, we address each component of the enterprise scaffold to help you successfully plan your Cloud migration and achieve the goals of the CRA.

5.3   The Enterprise Structure

At the foundation of the enterprise scaffold is a hierarchy that comes with your enterprise enrollment. The enterprise structure includes defining how Azure is organized within each department or line of business, and it reflects the need for billing, resources management, and resource access. In this section, we will address two types of hierarchies:

1. An **Enterprise Hierarchy** that reflects your cost model across corporate departments.
2. A **Management hierarchy** that helps you group subscriptions to enable more granular access control management and flexible approach for enforcing policies.

We will also address some design patterns that you can use when creating subscriptions, along with a proposed subscription model for myCloudCo.

5.3.1   Enterprise Hierarchy

When you start planning your enterprise hierarchy, think of cost and billing. Of course, there is a cost when you deploy and consume resources and services in the Cloud. It is not free. It is usually based on consumption. The more you consume, the more you pay.

Therefore, it is crucial to have a way to govern and manage your spending without slowing down business units from getting the promised value from using the Cloud and while ensuring compliance with a set of guidelines. You need two things to achieve this:

1. A way to manage cost across different organizational levels.
2. A concept of delegation to facilitate provisioning resources quickly in the Cloud through well-defined roles.

The foundation that Microsoft comes up with is a hierarchy and a relationship of the *Azure Enterprise Enrollment* through subscriptions and resource groups. In such hierarchy as shown in figure 5.5, you can divide your *enterprise agreement* into departments, accounts, and finally subscriptions and resource groups to match your organization's structure.

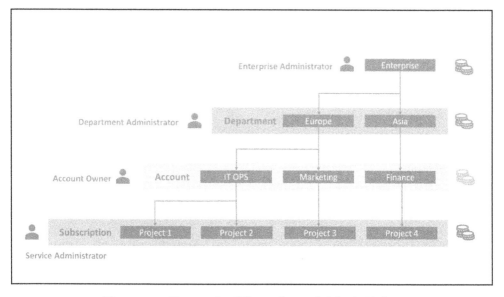

Figure 5.5 - Enterprise Hierarchy and Admin Roles

At the enterprise level, there is an **Enterprise Administrator**, the first account created at onboarding, who has full access and visibility across all resources of your enrollment. You can have multiple enterprise administrators per enrollment. This is when the hierarchy starts getting its shape.

The Enterprise Administrator can then create **Departments** depending on your organization's structure. You can have *departments* that reflect functions, business units, or geographies. There is also a **Department Administrator** for each *department* that you define.

Now each Department Administrator delegates the task of creating subscriptions to one or more **Account Owners**. Account Owners then create **Subscriptions**, and they (Account Owners) become the **Service Administrator** for subscriptions they create. Once a subscription is created, an *Account Owner* can delegate the role of *Service Administrator* to a developer or IT admin to start creating resources.

At each level, consumption and cost can be rolled up and isolated to get better visibility. As an example, an *Account Owner* can have visibility and resource consumption for all subscriptions she or he manages. Therefore, an *Account Owner* is financially responsible for all subscriptions she or he creates and manages.

Within each subscription, resources that share the same life cycle can be grouped under a **Resource Group**. A *Resource Group* is just a logical container that is used to assign policies and permissions. Table 20 lists the enterprise structure roles and their responsibilities.

Role	Responsibilities
Enterprise Administrator	First account created at onboarding. Full access and visibility into all activity and resources of a corporate enrollment.
Enterprise Administrator (read-only)	Read-only access to enterprise enrollment settings.
Departmental Administrator	Delegated by the enterprise administrator. Can create and have visibility into multiple account owners.
Department Administrator (read-only)	View department administrators and accounts in the department.
Account Owner	Delegated by a departmental administrator. Create and cancel subscriptions. Change the billing for a subscription. Manage all subscriptions in an account. Becomes the first service administrator on subscriptions.
Service Administrator	A classic subscription administrator role that is equivalent to the *Account Owner* role at the subscription scope in the new *Role-Based Access Control (RBAC)* model.

Table 5.2 - Enterprise Structure Roles

5.3.2   Management Hierarchy

We covered so far the *enterprise hierarchy*, which is formed with cost management in mind (billing hierarchy). But what if you want to group subscriptions differently to match your access management and policy enforcement needs, apart from how their consumption is managed?

You can use Azure **Management Groups** for that purpose. Each subscription can be a member of one *management group*, and *management groups* can be nested up to six levels. Therefore, you can group all subscriptions hosting production workloads (regardless of their location in the enterprise hierarchy) under one management group. By doing that, you get more granular access management and policy enforcement options. You can define access rules and *Azure Policies* at the management group level, and they will apply to all child subscriptions.

5.3.3 Subscription Design Patterns

Subscriptions are containers where all Cloud resources are contained regardless of their location. You can have resources from different regions under the same subscription. They are billing units; therefore, without a subscription, you cannot create resources.

You might be wondering: why don't you put all your resources inside one fat subscription? There are many reasons why this might be a bad idea. So, let's see what subscriptions represent in Azure. Subscriptions serve many purposes. They are *billing units*. You can roll up consumption at the subscription level. They are the *logical limit of scale* by which resources can be allocated. They also represent administration boundaries. You can assign admin roles at the subscription level.

When you think of subscriptions, consider how your deployments will scale if and when subscription limits are reached. For example, there is a logical limit on the number of cores a subscription can host. Therefore, scalability becomes a key factor when planning your subscription model.

Let's look at the following subscription design patterns.

- The *life cycle approach*, like separating the production environment in one subscription and other nonproduction environments (such as dev or QA) in other subscription(s). This creates a layer of isolation and gives you better control over changes in production environments.
- Creating a subscription per department or line-of-business unit, like grouping your marketing applications under one subscription and your HR workloads under a different one. You can also create separate subscriptions per geography if this fits your needs.
- Containment strategy can influence your subscription model as well. If you have a highly regulated environment (like hosting credit card

information), consider creating a separate subscription to isolate and contain that environment.

Let us now look at a couple of examples. The subscription model shown in figure 5.6 uses *one subscription per application* and a separate subscription to host infrastructure services like VPN gateways and domain controllers.

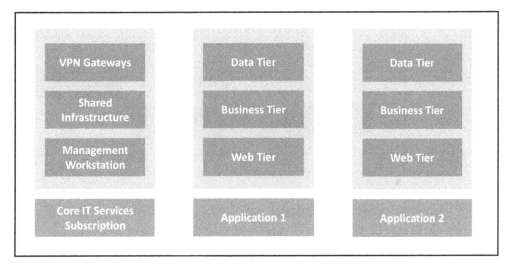

Figure 5.6 - Subscription Model 1

In another example, the subscription model shown in figure 5.7 extends the previous subscription model by separating the production environment from the dev and QA environments, so *each application needs three subscriptions*. Although having many subscriptions increases complexity and management costs, this model has many benefits, including:

- Separate teams have access to production and nonproduction environments.
- Dev and QA environments can scale independently from the production environment.
- Different sets of policies can be applied to production environments, such as setting an *Azure Resource Lock* at the subscription level to stop introducing changes.

In the same example, a management group can be defined to group subscriptions belonging to the same application, or separate management groups can be defined for production and nonproduction environments.

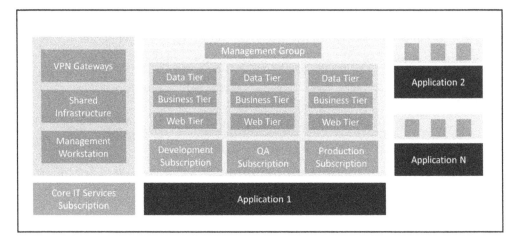

Figure 5.7 - Subscription Model 2

Another subscription model you can use is to group *production workloads* into one subscription and *nonproduction workloads* in a separate one, as shown in figure 5.8.

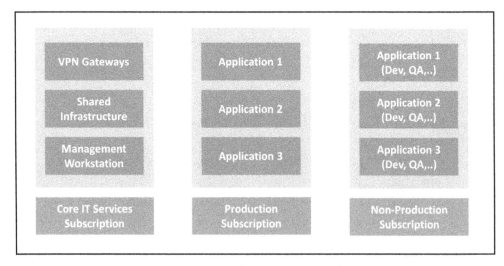

Figure 5.8 - Subscription Model 3

5.3.4 Proposed Enterprise Structure

It is time to define the *Enterprise Structure* for myCloudCo by defining their Enterprise Hierarchy, Management Hierarchy, and Subscription Model.

5.3.4.1 Proposed Enterprise Hierarchy

myCloudCo has an enterprise agreement with Microsoft, and part of its *enterprise enrollment*, an **Enterprise Administrator** account, is identified during enrollment. myCloudCo created additional Enterprise Administrator accounts to ensure one of their enterprise admins are available at any time.

Four departments are identified here: Marketing, Finance, HR, and IT. **Department Administrators** are also identified as the organization's CMO, CFO, CHO, and CTO, respectively.

Azure consumption is rolled up at the *department level*, so department heads can get visibility over their corresponding costs. Each Department Administrator delegates the responsibility for creating subscriptions to **Account Owners**. For example, the CTO is not going to create subscriptions himself. He might delegate this task to the DevOps manager for example.

Account Owners create subscriptions to host resources and become the **Service Administrator** for subscriptions they create. After the subscription is created, they delegate that Service Administrator role to the person responsible for creating resources and administering that subscription. Account Owners are financially responsible for the cost associated with subscriptions they create. Therefore, they keep track of the overall cost for all their subscriptions. Figure 5.9 shows the *proposed Enterprise Hierarchy* for myCloudCo.

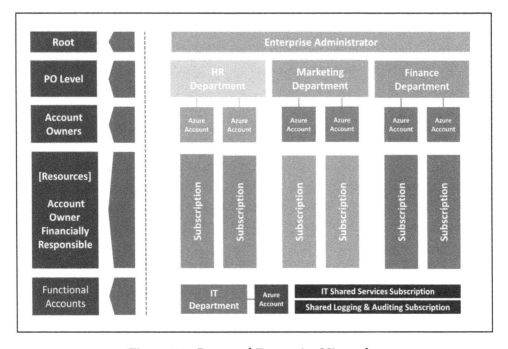

Figure 5.9 - Proposed Enterprise Hierarchy

5.3.4.2 Proposed Subscription Model

myCloudCo decided to implement a flexible and agile subscription model to empower its business units to deploy individual workloads in Azure while adhering to central IT policies. Each line-of-business (LOB) application represents a **Workspace** as shown in figure 5.10 that consists of three subscriptions: Production, Dev, and QA.

In this case, the Marketing Portal represents a separate **LOB workspace** with three subscriptions for each *environment*.

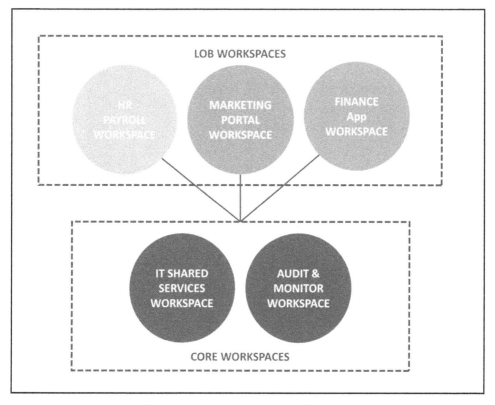

Figure 5.10 - Proposed Workspaces

Furthermore, all **Shared Infrastructure Services** (such as domain controllers and on-premises connectivity) are placed into a dedicated subscription. This eliminates the need to deploy such services inside each LOB subscription and provides better segregation of duties. Only central IT teams can manage the *shared infrastructure* resources hosted in the IT shared services subscription, while developers can manage resources hosted in their LOB subscriptions.

Moreover, for compliance and auditing needs, all *monitoring services and audit logs* from all subscriptions are hosted into a separate subscription. This way, access to read and manage audit logs across all workspaces can be restricted and managed separately.

We end up with three LOB workspaces. Each LOB workspace consists of three subscriptions, as shown in figure 5.11. There are also two core workspaces for shared infrastructure services and monitoring. In total, we have eleven subscriptions:

- Three subscriptions for the **Marketing Portal Workspace**
  - o myCloudCo Marketing Portal Production.
  - o myCloudCo Marketing Portal Dev.
  - o myCloudCo Marketing Portal QA.

- Three subscriptions for the **HR Payroll Workspace**
  - o myCloudCo HR Payroll Production.
  - o myCloudCo HR Payroll Dev.
  - o myCloudCo HR Payroll QA.

- Three subscriptions for the **Financial App Workspace**
  - o myCloudCo Finance App Production.
  - o myCloudCo Finance App Dev.
  - o myCloudCo Finance App QA.

- Two subscriptions of the two **Core Workspaces**
  - o myCloudCo IT Shared Services
  - o myCloudCo IT Auditing and Monitoring

You might be wondering, *"Why would you add your company name to your company's subscriptions? That seems a little overkill."* Well, there is a good reason for that, especially if a contractor from outside your company is helping you to deploy resources inside your subscription. The same contractor might be working on subscriptions from different companies, and when he logs into the Azure portal, he sees a list of all subscriptions he is associated with. If your company name is not part of your subscription name, the contractor might see two subscriptions called "HR Payroll Production" that belong to two different companies and might deploy resources in the wrong subscription.

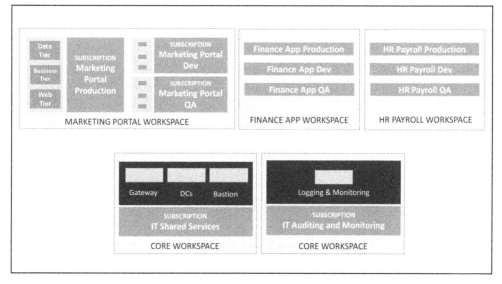

Figure 5.11 - Proposed Subscription Model

5.3.4.3 Proposed Management Hierarchy

To better manage subscriptions, myCloudCo decided to create *Management Groups* to easily group *production environments* separately from other environments. By default, there is one management group called "Root" that is created by default. Under this root management group, the following management groups are to be created, as shown in figure 5.12:

- Production Management Group.
- Dev Management Group.
- QA Management Group.
- Shared Services Management Group.
- Auditing and Monitoring Management Group.

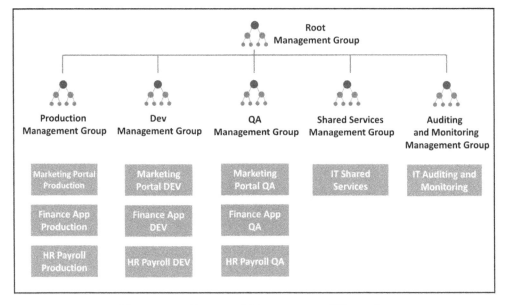

Figure 5.12- Proposed Management Hierarchy

5.4   Deployment Essentials

Once you planned your *Enterprise Structure* and before deploying resources, there are common best practices and concepts that are extremely important as they can influence your decision on where to migrate your data and how to deploy resources more efficiently.

We start with naming conventions for all your Cloud resources, resource groups, and subscriptions. After migration, you will end up with a lot of resources like network cards, load balancers, storage accounts, and more. Without a proper naming convention, you will end up with a big mess.

We also discuss automation and *Infrastructure as Code*. You can't keep doing things the old way by manually provisioning resources. The Cloud is a very dynamic environment, and changes happen all times. Using *templates* to deploy resources ensures consistency of your environment and solves the snowflake problem as changes accumulate over time without proper control.

Finally, which region should you use to host your data? Are you going to randomly pick a region and deploy resources there? In fact, there are couple of factors to consider, as explained in this section.

5.4.1   Naming Convention

A good naming convention helps you identify resources in the Azure portal, on a bill, and within scripts. It helps you remove the confusion when you create resources and reduce inconsistency in naming Cloud resources.

You might already have naming conventions for your on-premises resources, so when you start deploying Cloud resources, you should extend your naming convention to cover Cloud resources. Naming conventions are even more important in Cloud environments as everything is managed by code and resource name. Sometimes it is even hard to change the Cloud resource name afterward.

Some resources should have unique names globally, while others should have unique names within a scope. Some resources can only accept lowercase, while most resources restrict the type of characters allowed in their names. There are a lot of resource types in Azure, so start with commonly used resources and extend your naming conventions over time.

5.4.1.1   Best Practices

Here are some rules to consider when naming resources:

- Since some resources only allow lowercase, consider using lowercase always.
- Use hyphens when permitted.
- Prefix resources with the resource type.
- Use well-defined building blocks as described later in this section.

5.4.1.2   Defining the Building Blocks

Building blocks are just affixes that are used when naming resources. For example, myCloudCo identifies the following building blocks to help them name their resources:

- Environment.
- Location.
- Instance count (01, 02, etc.)

- Product or service.
- Role.

If you are including the product name as part of naming a resource, then how would you refer to the HR Payroll Application, for example? Is it going to be *"HRParyroll"*, *"Payroll"*, or *"HRApp"*? Same applies if you want to refer to the environment type. Is it *"Production"* or just *"Prod"*?

Let us start defining the building blocks for myCloudCo. Table 30 lists the **Environment Type** codes used as part of the resource name.

Environment Type	Code
Production	PR
Dev	DV
QA	QA
IT Core Services	MG

Table 5.3 - Naming Convention Building Blocks - Environment Type

Since myCloudCo is planning to deploy resources in the United States only, they created a naming convention for Azure regions in the United States only. Table 30 lists suggested **Azure Region** codes used as part of the resource name.

Azure Region	Code
US East	USE1
US East2	USE2
US Central	USC1
US West	USW1
US West 2	USW2

Table 5.4 - Naming Convention Building Blocks - Azure Regions

There is also a need perhaps to include the *workload role* as part of the resource name. Table 40 lists **Workload Role** codes used as part of the resource name.

Workload Role	Code
Database	DB
Application	AP
Web Server	WS
Infrastructure	IN
Messaging	MS

Table 5.5 - Naming Convention Building Blocks - Workload Roles

Another commonly used element to include in the naming convention is to include the *service type* the resource is serving. Table 50 lists **Service Type** codes used as part of the resource name.

Service Type	Code
Management Server (Infrastructure)	MG
Firewall Device (Infrastructure)	FW
Bastions (Infrastructure)	BST
Domain Controllers (Infrastructure)	DC
Infrastructure Services (Infrastructure)	INF
Load Balancer (Infrastructure)	LB
Finance Workload (Application)	FIN
Marketing Portal Workload (Application)	MAR
HR Payroll Workload (Application)	HR

Table 5.6 - Naming Convention Building Blocks - Services

You probably see people using the workload tier as part of their naming convention. Table 60 lists the **Workload Tier** codes used as part of the resource name.

Workload Tier	Code
Data	DB
Business	AP

Web	WS
DMZ	DMZ
Management	MG

Table 5.7 - Naming Convention Building Blocks - Workload Tiers

5.4.1.3 Resource Tags

As you add resources to subscriptions, you should tag them for better cost management and operational purposes. Start by identifying all enterprise-level tags that you will use consistently across subscriptions before creating resources.

Tags are nothing more than metadata associated with Cloud resources. *Tag keys* can be 512 characters; *tag values* can be up to 256 characters. You can apply resource tags to resource groups and resources, but keep in mind that a tag assigned to a resource group will not be inherited by resources inside that resource group. You can also add up to fifteen resource tags to the same resource or resource group.

Again, why should you tag resources? Well, they help you organize all deployed resources and they definitely become handy in billing and cost management as you can get aggregated cost for all resources with the same tag.

myCloudCo decided to use resource tags to manage the cost associated with different projects and to perform auditing (who is the owner of each resource). *Azure Policies* are used later to enforce the use of resource tags across all deployed resources. Here is a list of tags that will be used:

- Project.
- Department.
- Cost Center (who is paying for the Azure consumption).
- Creator or Owner
- Environment (production, dev, QA).

With these tags, myCloudCo can get the cost of all production workloads across all subscriptions by just filtering by tag value.

5.4.1.4 Naming Subscriptions

Start with a naming convention for your subscriptions as they are the first thing you will create. Make sure your subscription name is clearly identifiable. Here is the naming convention myCloudCo will be using:

<Company> <Department (optional)>
<Product (optional)> <Environment>

For example, *"myCloudCo Marketing Portal Dev"* is the name of the subscription that will host the dev environment for the marketing portal.

5.4.1.5 VNET Naming Convention

For naming VNETs, myCloudCo uses the following naming convention:

VNET-<Region Code>-<Count (01, 02 ...)>-<Environment>

For example, *"VNET-USE1-01-PR"* is the name of a VNET used for a production environment in US East region.

5.4.1.6 Subnet Naming Convention

For naming Subnets, myCloudCo uses the following naming convention:

SUBNET-<Region Code>-<Tier>-<Count
(01, 02 ...)>-<Environment>

For example, *"SUBNET-USE2-MG-01-PR"* is the name of a subnet in US East 2 region that is used to host management workloads (e.g., domain controllers) and is used for production environment.

5.4.1.7 Server Naming Convention

For naming Virtual Machines, myCloudCo uses the following naming convention:

<Region Code><Service><Role><Count><Environment>

For example, *"USE1FINDB01PR"* is the name of a financial application database server in the US East 1 region located in a production environment.

5.4.1.8 VNET Peering Naming Convention

For naming VNET Peering Connections, myCloudCo uses the following naming convention:

PVNET-<Source VNET>-<Target VNET>

For example, *"PNET-VNET-USE1-01-PR-VNET-USE1-02-PR"* is a name of a peering connection between two VNETs.

5.4.1.9 NIC Adapter Naming Convention

For naming NIC Adapters, myCloudCo uses the following naming convention:

<Host Name>-NIC-<Count>

5.4.1.10 Virtual Gateways Naming Convention

For naming Virtual Gateways, myCloudCo uses the following naming convention:

VNG-<Region>-<Destination>-<Count>-<Type>

Destination can be simply *"on premises"* or a specific physical on-premises site in case multiple connections to different on-premises locations are required. The type is either *"EX"* for ExpressRoute or *"VPN"* for a VPN connection.

5.4.1.11 Route Table Naming Convention

For naming Route Tables, myCloudCo uses the following naming convention:

RT-<Region>-<Tier>-<Count>-<Environment>

For example, *"RT-USE1-DATA-01-PR"* is a route table applied at the data tier for a production environment in the US East 1 region.

5.4.1.12 Network Security Group Naming Convention

For naming Network Security Groups, myCloudCo uses the following naming convention:

NSG-<Tier>-<SUBNET | Service>-<Count>-<Environment>

For example, *"NSG-DATA-SUBNET-01-DEV"* is a network security group assigned at the data subnet in the development environment. A region code can also be included in the name. Another example would be *"NSG-MG-BST-01-PR"*, which is a network security group applied to the bastion host itself.

5.4.1.13 Load Balancer Naming Convention

For naming Load Balancers, myCloudCo uses the following naming convention:

LB-<Region>-<Tier>-<EXT | INT>-<Service>-<Count>-<Environment>

For example, *"LB-USE1-WEB-EXT-FIN-01-PR"*, which is an external load balancer in the US East 1 region, that is used in the financial application production environment.

5.4.1.14 Availability Set Naming Convention

For naming Availability Sets, myCloudCo uses the following naming convention:

AS-\<Region\>-\<Service\>-\<Count\>-\<Environment\>

For example, *"AS-USE1-DC-01-MG"* is an availability set for domain controllers provisioned in the management environment inside US East 1 region.

5.4.1.15 Storage Account Naming Convention

For naming storage accounts, keep in mind that storage account names should be unique across all Azure and can only contain lowercase letters and numbers. myCloudCo uses the following naming convention:

sa\<Region\>\<Service\>\<Environment\>\<Count\>\<[s] for standard | [p] for premium\>

For example, *"sause1mgpr01s"* is a standard storage account that is used for network logging purposes in US East 1 region.

5.4.1.16 Resource Group Naming Convention

For naming Resource Groups, myCloudCo uses the following naming convention:

RG-\<Service\>-\<Count\>-\<Environment\>

For example, *"RG-INF-01-MG"* could be a resource group hosting virtual network resources. Since resource groups may contain resources from different Azure regions, the **\<Region\>** is not used within the name.

5.4.2   Where to Migrate

You should decide early where will you host your data. Sometimes many organizations overlook choosing the right region as they don't understand the benefits and/or consequences related. Many Cloud providers maintain data centers in different geographies and might give you the option to pick which data center hosts your data. Here are some factors to consider when picking an Azure region.

5.4.2.1 Data Sovereignty

Provisioning resources in the Cloud is easy for most organizations. But things can be complicated when you are a regulated industry and dealing with data that is subject to local and international regulations, like credit card information and Personally Identifiable Data (PII). What seems like an easy task of just adding storage to data centers is now much more complex, especially when data is hosted in the Cloud outside traditional IT procurement and operations channels.

5.4.2.2 Proximity to Customers

Another factor to consider is latency, as you want to deploy resources and services closest to most of your customers whenever possible. If most of your customers are in the United States, then it wouldn't be a good choice to host your Cloud resources in Europe, for example. As proximity to customers is very important, some organizations might choose to deploy their applications across different regions and use special types of *geo load balancers* to serve customers from the nearest region.

5.4.2.3 Service Availability

The availability of Azure services varies by region and whether the service is currently in "preview" or "generally available." If you are planning to deploy M-services VMs, it might not be available in all Azure regions, for example. Moreover, some organizations might consider deploying dedicated hardware security module (HSMs) for compliance and security needs. Since HSM is not offered in all Azure regions, this can be a deciding factor also.

5.4.2.4 Restriction

Some Azure regions have restrictions such as the billing address of the customer. Australian regions, for example, can only be used by customers with billing addresses in Australia or New Zealand. This might change with time, but it is worth checking the official documentation for any restrictions before picking a region.

5.4.2.5 Pricing

The cost of services within different Azure regions is not necessarily the same, as it is controlled by many factors. If latency, compliance, and governance are not influencing your decision, it may be best to deploy in the region with the lowest cost.

5.4.2.6 Paired Regions

Paired regions are Azure regions that are in the same geography but are at least three hundred miles apart, which can be a great choice for deploying cross-region services and application while maintaining geographic residency.

If you are planning to deploy workloads across two Azure regions, it is recommended to consider paired Azure regions. This is because Microsoft ensures that sequential updates occur across paired regions. Also, when Microsoft is recovering from regional recovery in the event of outage, it takes into consideration paired regions so that at least one of the paired regions is recovered with priority.

Furthermore, by deploying resources across paired regions, you can take advantage of active-passive deployment pattern with low latency to the second region for rapid recovery in case of a disaster.

As you can see, there is a lot to think about before choosing an Azure region. It can be very hard to migrate your workloads to another region afterward, so plan this very carefully.

5.4.3   Infrastructure as Code

Moving to the Cloud unlocks many opportunities for all businesses. Data centers are built using SDNs, and anything you do in the Cloud can be executed through well-defined APIs. Since everything is defined in software, there is an opportunity for doing things differently and perhaps saving time and effort.

5.4.3.1 Addressing the Problem

Traditionally, you configure your infrastructure and deploy different services, and everything works just fine. But there are always going to be changes that you introduce to your current infrastructure to solve a business or security needs, and every time you go and change something in a production environment, you create a snowflake, that is, a unique configuration that cannot be reproduced automatically.

What started as a well-documented and compliant environment is now an accumulation of changes performed by different people over time, and what you had considered a compliant environment becomes a different one over time. Take, for example, someone who deployed something and leaves the company, leaving you and your teams with no clue of what was changed.

But there is good news. Cloud infrastructure is moving from being physical to being a software that can be managed differently and with version control. Think about the time you need to provision a server or even create a new production environment that looks like your development one.

What if you want to deploy your applications in another Azure region? How much time does it take you to build the same infrastructure? And when you do so, will it look exactly like the original one?

A better way to deploy resources in the Cloud is by taking advantage of its capabilities and using a declarative way to provision your infrastructure. This is called **Infrastructure as Code (IaC).**

5.4.3.2 What Is It?

Infrastructure as Code (IaC) is the management of infrastructure (networks, VMs, load balancers, and connection topology) in a descriptive model, using the same versioning as the DevOps team uses for source code.

Just think about the possibilities and benefits, like reducing provisioning time, for example. Every time you want to migrate or deploy a new LOB application, you run a piece of code that creates a similar standardized and compliant environment like the one you use in other LOB environments. It gives you the testable and repeatable pattern that you need in a dynamic environment like the Cloud.

Not only is it a faster way, you can also rely less on the availability of the person who deployed your environment, even if that individual leaves the company. It gives you a single source of truth of what your environment always looks like.

Also, what can be better: giving your auditors a document that describes your environment that might be different at audit time or a declarative truth about what the environment looks like now?

5.4.3.3 Automate Deployments to Azure

With Azure, you can use **Azure Templates** (JSON templates) to provision your applications using a declarative way so you use the same template to repeatedly deploy your application during every stage of the application life cycle.

You can also use *PowerShell scripts* to deploy resources using code. The difference is that the PowerShell approach focuses more on individual resources, whereas *Azure Templates* focus more on groups of related resources.

As a best practice for production subscriptions and resource groups, your goal should be to prevent admins and developers from touching the Azure portal to interactively configure resources. This level of DevOps takes a concerted effort, and you should invest time in training your teams to use automation during your Cloud migration journey.

Remember, it is not just migrating workloads to the Cloud. It is utilizing the new capabilities offered by the Cloud to reduce cost and effort as much as possible.

5.4.4   Automation

As you may know, an organization's maturity is sometimes measured by the level of automation they have incorporated. Automation is a full-time job and one of the most important operation tasks within your Cloud team. It is the connective tissue of your enterprise scaffold that links each area together and is deeply associated with the *IaC* concept.

When you think about automation, consider how much time and cost you can optimize. You can optimize your cost by using automation along with *IaC* to resize resources, scale up/down, and turn off unused machines. With automation, you can also optimize operations by gaining a level of repeatability, which in turn increases availability and security and enables your teams to focus on solving business problems.

5.5   Identity and Access Management

Now it is time to ask yourself, *"Who should have access to resources?"* and *"How do you control this access?"* More importantly, *"Which service is going to authenticate users?"*

On the other hand, security best practices like *separation of duties* and the *principle of least privilege* are also worth considering in the Cloud. These principles are not only used for your on-premises infrastructure. You should also apply them when planning your identity and access management in the Cloud.

5.5.1   Subscriptions and Azure AD

Let's start with this statement, *"Azure Active Directory (Azure AD) is the identity and access management service for Azure resources and subscriptions"*. In other words, Azure AD authenticates any access to Azure resources and the Azure management portal.

In fact, when you sign up for a Cloud service, an *organization object* is created that represents your company, typically identified by one of more public DNS names (such as myCloudCo.com), as shown in figure 5.13. An *organization object* is created when you sign up for Office 365, Azure, or other Cloud services like Intune. When using Azure, the *Organization* is the container for subscriptions.

Now a subscription is an agreement you make with Microsoft to use one or more of their Cloud offerings for which charges accrue based on either a per-user license fee or on Cloud-based resource consumption. Users who consume Microsoft Cloud services are stored in an *Azure AD Tenant*, which can be synchronized with your existing on-premises directory.

Now that we understand how Azure AD fits in the picture, let's see how Azure AD and subscriptions are related. Each Azure subscription *trusts one* Azure AD instance, and multiple subscriptions can trust the same Azure AD instance. Azure AD is what your subscriptions use to authenticate users when they access resources and change Cloud resource configuration.

If one of your subscriptions expire, then access to resources associated with the subscription stops. But the Azure AD directory remains in Azure and can be associated to another subscription.

Getting back to our example, myCloudCo decided to synchronize their on-premises Active Directory with Azure AD so they can assign users to roles using their on-premises identities.

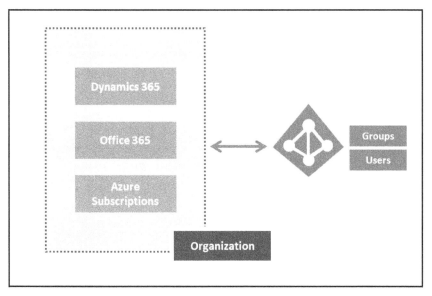

Figure 5.13 - Azure AD and Azure Subscriptions Relationship

5.5.2 Azure RBAC

Now that we established the relationship between Azure AD and Azure subscriptions, we have addressed the *authentication* part. Once users are authenticated, how can we restrict what users can do after they authenticate? That is, how do we solve the *authorization* part?

Authorization and access management for Azure resources are enforced using **Azure Role-Based Access Control** (**RBAC**). Within Azure RBAC, there are many roles that represent collection of actions that a role can perform. The *Virtual Machine Contributor* role, for example, allows the user to create and manage VMs. If you want to assign a role for a user or a group, which is also known as a **Role Assignment**, then you should specify three things:

- Which users or groups (**who**).
- What role to be assigned (**what** actions are allowed).
- The scope of role assignment (**where**), which can be:
  - At the *Resource* level.
  - At the *Resource Group* level.
  - At the *Subscription* level.
  - Or at the *Management Group* level.

Azure AD is used for authentication, while *Azure RBAC* facilitates authorization and access management for Azure resources. *Role Assignment* is adding a user/group to a role (set of actions) and specifying a scope.

5.5.3   Azure AD Roles vs. Azure RBAC

Azure RBAC roles are not the only roles that you should worry about. Azure AD itself has many built-in roles that are separate from the roles defined within Azure RBAC. While Azure RBAC defines roles to manage Azure resources, Azure AD roles are used to manage your Azure AD instance itself. Azure AD roles used to manage Azure AD are not related to Azure RBAC roles used to manage access to Azure subscriptions and resources.

Figure 5.14 shows both Azure RBAC roles and Azure AD roles as well as their assignment levels. The most important Azure AD role you should carefully manage is the *Global Administrator* role, as it is considered the most powerful role in Azure AD. You should not login with this account except for emergency situations.

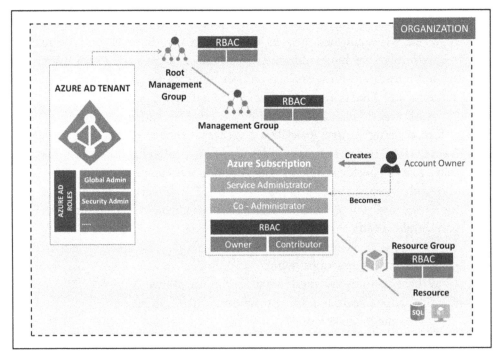

Figure 5.14 - Azure AD Roles vs Azure RBAC Roles

5.5.4   Management Roles

Now it is time to think about how to assign your users to different roles defined in Azure RBAC. Remember that myCloudCo has already identified different teams that will manage their Cloud infrastructure *(SecOps, NetOps, SysOps, and DevOps)*.

There could be different sets of these teams managing separate LOB workspaces. For example, there could be *SecOps, NetOps, SysOps, and DevOps* teams managing the Marketing Portal subscriptions, while different *SecOps, NetOps, SysOps, and DevOps* teams manage the Financial Application subscriptions. It all depends on your organization structure and preference.

To distinguish between teams managing different applications, you can name your teams as (*App*SecOps, *App*NetOps, *App*SysOps, and *App*DevOps), where *"App"* is replaced with the LOB application name.

myCloudCo decided to have the same *SecOps, NetOps, and SysOps* teams managing all subscriptions and two sets of *DevOps* teams. One *DevOps* team is responsible for deploying resources in the *dev* and *QA* environments (called *NonProDevOps* team), and a different *DevOps* team is responsible for deploying resources in the production environments (called *ProDevOps* team).

Figure 5.15 shows myCloudCo teams and their RBAC assignment scope. Keep in mind that *DevOps* teams should not have rights (perhaps only read) on the Core Subscriptions (*"IT Shared Services"* and the *"IT Auditing and Monitoring"* Subscriptions).

Assigning Azure RBAC permissions at the management group level is a recommended option. When you create a new subscription and add it to a management group, it automatically gets all assigned Azure RBAC permissions and *Azure Policies* applied at the management group level. Therefore, you don't need to separately manage Azure RBAC permissions for each subscription you create.

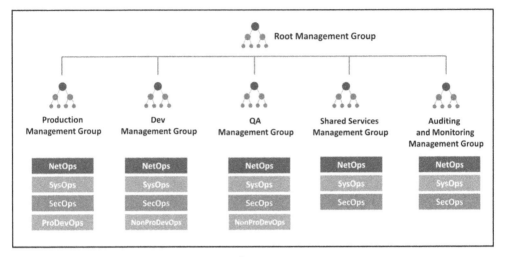

Figure 5.15 - Proposed RBAC Assignment Scope

5.5.5 Separation of Duties and Principle of Least Privilege

Separation of Duties is an important information security concept, which ensures that any significant change to infrastructure involves multiple roles. For a major change to happen, more than one person must review and approve a change.

The subscription model proposed previously for myCloudCo introduces the *"IT Shared Services"* subscription, which is a separate subscription that central IT teams manage, and it hosts common infrastructure and security services like connectivity to on-premises network and bastion workstations. Other LOB subscriptions can use the VPN gateway in the *"IT Shared Services"* subscription to connect to on-premises network instead of implementing a separate VPN gateway for each subscription.

This creates the ground for a perfect *Separation-of-Duties* model. Central IT teams can focus on managing resources in the *"IT Shared Services"* subscription, while software developers are given control over their LOB subscriptions without compromising security or interfering with networking infrastructure.

The *Principle of Least Privilege* is also used here. A developer who is working on developing the HR payroll system, for example, should not have the right to change firewall configuration in the *"IT Shared*

Services" subscription. Of course, all this requires proper planning for all management roles in advance and defining responsibilities that meets your security, compliance, and policies in place.

5.5.6   Secure Identities

What about compromised credentials, the use of weak passwords, and users with standing admin rights? No matter how well you plan your authentication and authorization structure, if your IT teams use weak passwords, someone can easily attack their credentials and compromise your whole Cloud infrastructure.

You can do a lot of things to mitigate this risk. First, you should require multifactor authentication (MFA) for all users who are managing Azure resources and Azure AD. Azure MFA can be used for this purpose.

Next, you should have a mechanism to monitor, track, and govern the use of administrative privileges in the Cloud by using a Privileged Account Management (PAM) system. **Azure Privileged Identity Management (Azure PIM)** is a great choice that is worth looking at. When configured properly, you can use *just-in-time (JIT)* admin role assignments instead of permanent assignments.

With JIT, eligible admins should activate their roles before using them, and when they do so, they are active in their admin role for a short period of time, depending on the task at hand. Figure 5.16 shows the main components of Azure PIM.

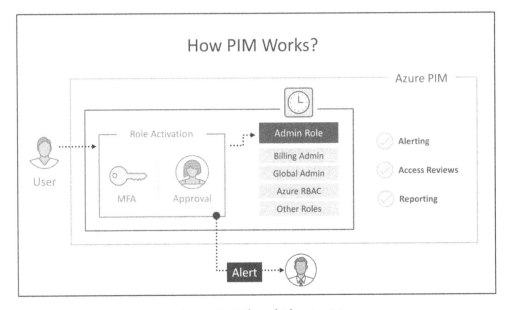

Figure 5.16 - Azure Privileged Identity Management

5.6   Core Networking

How will your users access Cloud workloads, and how can you secure this access? Are they going to use your corporate internal network to do so? Is external access through the internet allowed? After all, it is easy for users to inadvertently put resources in the wrong spot and potentially open them to malicious access.

What you need is appropriate controls in place to ensure users make the right decisions. To establish governance at the networking level, you can implement many core resources like virtual networks, user-defined routes (UDRs), virtual network peering, service endpoints, network security groups, and specialized network virtual appliances (NVAs).

But let us step back and think about the big picture for a moment. You need to think about some design objectives that guide your networking implementation. You need to consider supporting multiple LOB applications in the Cloud, while ensuring isolation and security but also flexibility. It should be easy to add or migrate more LOB applications without affecting existing Cloud workloads. For example, adding a new LOB application should not require any changes to existing LOB applications (isolation concept).

From the other side, you should be able to remove or delete LOB application without affecting existing Cloud workloads. In other words, you don't want your deployed LOB applications to depend on each other from a networking and security perspective.

Even within the same LOB application, different tiers (web, business, and data tiers) should be isolated to a certain extent. The web tier should not communicate directly with the data tier; only the business tier can do so.

In this section, we cover how to properly plan your core Cloud networking and establish governance at different levels. There are a lot of best practices that you can consider when planning your core networking infrastructure. So, let's get started.

5.6.1 The Virtual Data Center

Up till now, we talked about many components to be addressed before deploying Cloud workloads. We talked about the billing and management hierarchies, and we addressed key deployment essentials like automation and naming conventions. We also talked about how to think of and plan your identity and access management and how on-premises identities can be synced to the Cloud.

But we didn't deploy anything yet. In fact, all what we did so far is preparation work to reach this moment where you can start imagining how your on-premises data center can be extended to the Cloud. You can think of the Cloud as one of your data centers, but a virtual one that is built on SDN and managed through a set of APIs.

If you are following up with what was covered so far in this chapter, you will quickly realize that establishing an *enterprise scaffold* is in fact a way to extend and maintain trust and governance in the Cloud. This approach is sometimes called the *Trusted Data Center Extension Model*.

With a proper *enterprise scaffold* and trust, the Cloud becomes just another data center, a virtual data center. Think of the virtual data center as your isolated Cloud within Azure. Within this space, you can build virtual boundaries (walls) and implement security controls. You can define network policies and establish compliance by carefully planning each component of your virtual data center.

A key takeaway from this section is to understand that the *virtual data center* concept is a way to imagine how to deploy your application estate in the Cloud while preserving key aspects of your current IT governance and taking advantage of the Cloud computing's agility.

5.6.2   Shared IT Security and Management Services

The most important concept that we address in this section is the *shared services model*. Simply put, you create a separate environment—we call it *"IT Shared Services"* environment—to host all shared services that other deployed LOB applications need to consume. This *IT Shared Services* environment is where all network traffic flows, policies are set, and core monitoring occurs.

By grouping all shared services in a separate environment (and possibly separate subscription), LOB environments and developers don't need to implement such common services and can instead consume these common services from the *IT Shared Services* environment *as a service* offered by the SecOps and NetOps teams. This model has many advantages such as:

- Developers can focus on deploying LOB applications without worrying about implementing services already offered by the *IT Shared Services* environment.
- Adding a new LOB application becomes a relatively smooth process, as all shared IT services (such as connectivity to on-premises and identity infrastructure) are already offered centrally.
- This model creates abstraction and isolation structures, where different sets of teams (SecOps and NetOps) manage sensitive security and management services in the *IT Shared Services* environment. Developers (DevOps teams) do not manage or have access to change such centralized IT services, which serves both the *separation-of-duties* principle and the *principle of least privilege*.

The *IT Shared Services* environment is implemented as a separate subscription that consists of a separate **Hub Virtual Network** that connects to other parts of the virtual data center as shown in figure 5.17. It also hosts and manages external connections used by resources hosted outside the virtual data center and facilitates on-premises connectivity. The *IT Shared Services* environment (which also can be called the *Hub VNET*) usually includes the following components:

- Gateways to connect to on-premises networks.
- Any connection from and to the internet.
- A central *hub virtual network*, through which all traffic between Cloud workloads and the on-premises network must pass.
- Central firewall to inspect and redirect traffic passing through the virtual data center to an on-premises network.
- Bastion workstation(s) used to manage resources in the virtual data center.
- Management services like domain controllers, DNS servers, FTP transfer servers, or PKI servers.
- Other shared resources and operation tools, such as code repositories or file servers.

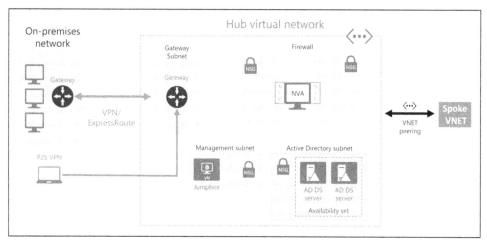

Figure 5.17 - Hub Network

5.6.3   LOB Application Workspaces

The design also calls for isolated environments to host various LOB applications (*LOB Workspaces*). Each LOB application has its own virtual network(s) and well-defined role assignments. LOB applications are the *spokes* in this *hub-and-spoke* model. The hub, of course, is the *IT Shared Services* environment.

Within each spoke virtual network, three different subnets are defined for each workload tier (*data tier subnet, business tier subnet, and web tier subnet*). Data flow between subnets is managed through Azure Network Security Groups (NSG) at the subnet level.

Each spoke (LOB VNET) has a *VNET Peering* configured with the central *Hub VNET* to consume shared IT services and facilitate connectivity with on-premises networks as shown in figure 18.

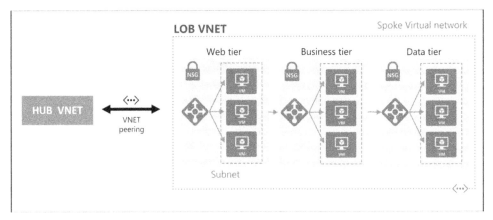

Figure 5.18 - Spoke Network

5.6.4   Central Firewall

Now that we have introduced the *hub-and-spoke* connectivity model, you should start addressing data exfiltration. Since DevOps teams are given control over their *Spoke VNETs (LOB VNETs)*, your central IT teams (SecOps and NetOps) need a way to enforce security controls and monitor traffic passing from and to *Spoke VNETs*.

The *Hub VNET* is the perfect place to do so since all traffic passing between *Spoke VNETs* and your on-premises networks or even between

Spoke VNETs should pass through the *Hub VNET*. This is enforced by configuring *User-Defined Routes (UDRs)* on spoke VNET subnets.

The next thing is to place a firewall using one or more *Network Virtual Appliances (NVAs)* in the *Hub VNET*, and all traffic from spoke virtual networks must pass through it. Through this central firewall, your SecOps team controls the traffic allowed to pass in and out of the virtual data center and determines how the traffic is directed.

If you are expecting a large amount of traffic between your on-premises network and workloads hosted in the virtual data center, it is better to deploy multiple firewall NVA devices and place two load balancers using the *high-availability ports* feature to distribute the traffic, as shown in figure 5.19. A front-end load balancer handles traffic going to spoke VNETs from on-premises network; a back-end load balancer handles traffic going from spoke VNETs to the on-premises network.

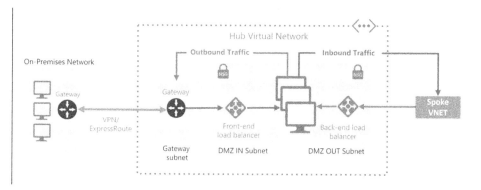

Figure 5.19 - Hub Central Firewall

5.6.5   On-Premises Connectivity

If you are planning to connect your on-premises networks to your virtual data center, you have two methods:

- **ExpressRoute**: This uses a dedicated private connection, usually facilitated by a connectivity provider.
- **Site-to-site VPN**: Using Azure VPN gateways, you can create a site-to-site connection and establish encrypted tunnel between your

on-premises network and your virtual data center over the public internet.

The gateway from Azure side is configured in a *Gateway Subnet* of the hub virtual network. The *Gateway Subnet* implements the following User-Defined Routes (UDRs) as shown in figure 5.20:

- Requests for spoke resources are routed through the central firewall.
- Requests for remote access to configured resources are sent to the jumpboxes in the management subnet.
- Requests for domain controllers and DNS services are sent to the AD subnet.

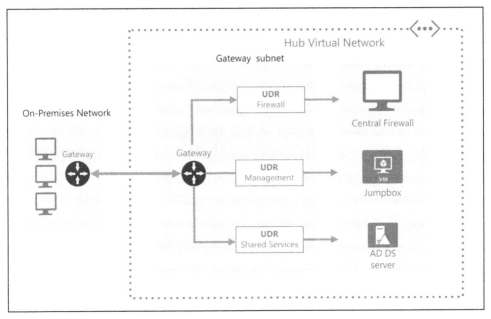

Figure 5.20 - Gateway Subnet UDRs

5.6.6   Internet Connectivity

Whenever there is a need to route traffic from or to the public internet, you should implement a full separate DMZ implementation. It is highly recommended to use one set of NVAs for traffic originated from internet and another set of NVAs for traffic originating from on premises.

Using only one set of firewalls for both is a security risk as it provides no security perimeter between the two sets of network traffic. Separating the two data flows reduces the complexity of checking security rules and makes it clear which rules correspond to which incoming network request.

Figure 5.21 shows an implementation of a separate DMZ that is used to handle internet traffic. You can deploy Azure Firewall, Web Application Firewall (WAF), or specialized NVA devices to handle internet traffic. The solution calls for two subnets. "**Public DMZ In**" subnet receives traffic originating from internet; "**Public DMZ Out**" subnet receives traffic originating from spoke virtual networks.

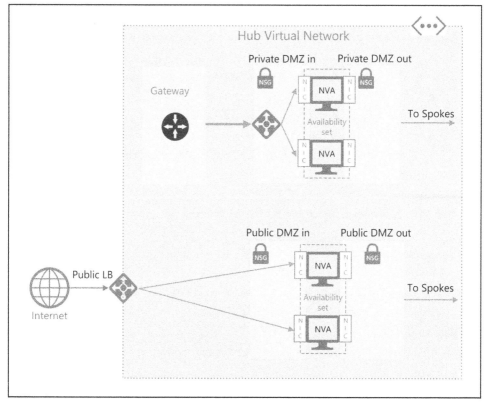

Figure 5.21 - Hub Public DMZ

Another decision you need to make is deciding how your Azure resources are going to access the public internet. By default, resources can access the internet without any special configuration, but you might want all internet traffic originating from your virtual data center to pass through your on-premises network for inspection. This is called *Forced Tunneling*. Without forced tunneling, internet-bound traffic from your VMs in Azure always traverse from Azure network infrastructure directly out to the internet.

5.6.7   Name Resolution and Domain Controllers

As part of your core network design, you should plan for a naming resolution within your Azure VNETs. By default, Azure DNS provides a naming resolution for all resources within a VNET. However, name resolution across VNETs is not available.

Furthermore, you might want all your VMs in Azure to be domain-joined to your on-premises AD to enforce your policies using group policies. Therefore, you can deploy two domain controllers in a separate subnet of the *Hub VNET* and configure a new AD site. The two domain controllers are placed in their own availability set and configured as the DNS servers for all VMs in the virtual data center. It is important to assign static IP addresses to domain controllers as they host the DNS services used by all VMs.

5.6.8   Administration and Management

It is recommended to deploy a jumpbox (bastion host) device(s) in a separate subnet (management subnet) of the *Hub VNET*. The jumpbox is used to manage and configure the central firewall and oversee other management tasks in the *Hub VNET* that are not available through the Azure portal.

The same jumpbox is also used to manage resources in spoke virtual networks, or you can configure a management subnet in each spoke with one or more jumpboxes. There are a couple of recommendations when it comes to deploying jumpboxes:

- It is highly recommended not to create public IP addresses for the jumpbox; instead you can use the on-premises connectivity to access it.

- Traffic coming from on premises to the management subnet (where the jumpbox is located) is routed directly through the gateway using UDRs configured on the gateway subnet without passing though the hub central firewall. There is a good reason for doing so. The jumpbox is the only device allowed to manage the central firewall, so if there is a problem with that firewall, access to the management subnet should still be available to fix the firewall configuration.
- NSG rules are applied to the management subnet to restrict access to specific IPs on the on-premises network.
- You should deploy at least two jumpboxes in the management subnet as an availability set.
- VM *Just-in time JIT* access is configured to restrict access to the jumpbox.

Moreover, you can implement the following controls for lock down jumpboxes:

- Azure Antimalware extension.
- Azure diagnostics extension.
- Azure monitoring agent.
- Azure Disk Encryption using Azure Key Vault.
- An *auto-shutdown policy* to reduce consumption of VM resources when not in use.
- Windows Defender Credential Guard enabled so that credentials and other secrets run in a protected environment that is isolated from the running operating system.

5.6.9   Special Considerations

There are some important technical constrains when deploying workloads in Azure. First, broadcast traffic is not allowed inside Azure VNETs. Moreover, multicast traffic is also not supported. If you are considering deploying any service that depends on broadcast and multicast, you should think twice.

Running some Microsoft Server software in Azure VM environment is not supported as well. For example, you can't run multipath I/O, Peer

Name Resolution Protocol, SNMP services, RRAS, or DHCP. A full list can be found at Microsoft official documentation.

5.6.10 IP Address Assignment

When it comes to assigning IP addresses, make sure to avoid overlapping IP addresses used for your virtual data center with your on-premises IP addresses or else routing becomes a problem. Keep also in mind that when you create subnets in Azure, there are five reserved addresses for each subnet:

- X:X:X.0: Network address.
- X:X:X.1: Reserved by Azure for the VNET router.
- X:X:X.2: Reserved by Azure for gateway use.
- X:X:X.3: Reserved by Azure for gateway use.
- X:X:X.255: Network broadcast address. Azure does not support broadcast in a VNET; therefore, this address is reserved.

5.6.11 Proposed Networking Infrastructure

Let us look at the proposed network layout for myCloudCo. Figure 5.22 shows the proposed **LOB Workspace** *(spoke)* networking setup. A Network Security Group (NSG) is configured on all three subnets to restrict traffic between tiers (web, business and data tiers). The *business tier* blocks all traffic that doesn't originate in the *web tier*, and the *data tier* blocks all traffic that doesn't originate in the *business tier*.

Application Security Groups (ASGs) are used to allow granular access to applications or groups of applications. This helps to identify resources by tag instead of listing IP addresses in a Network Security Group.

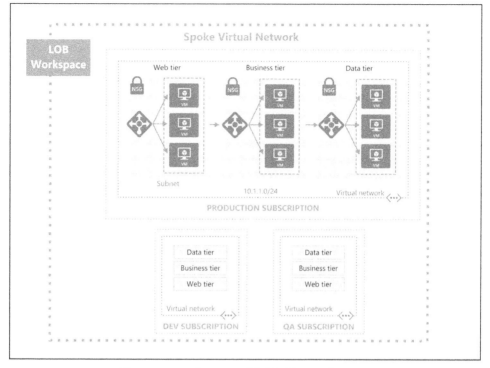

Figure 5.22 - Proposed LOB Network Setup

Figure 5.23 shows the proposed network setup for the **Hub Virtual Network** (*IT Shared Services* environment). To support remote users, a *point-to-site* client VPN is used.

myCloudCo plans to deploy an ExpressRoute connection, which offers more reliability, faster speeds, and lower latencies. Since ExpressRoute might take time to deploy, a *site-to-site* VPN Gateway will be deployed to quickly start using Azure resources. Once the ExpressRoute connection is in place, VPN Gateway is going to be used as a failover connection in case the ExpressRoute goes down.

myCloudCo decided to use *force tunneling* to better inspect and regulate traffic going to the internet by defining UDRs on all spoke subnets. In case of ExpressRoute, this needs some additional configurations from the service provider side.

A separate DMZ is configured for traffic originated from the internet that is used to publish the *Marketing Portal* application. Since myCloudCo wants to deploy the *Marketing Portal* application across two Azure regions, *Azure Front Door* is used to distribute traffic across the two Azure regions.

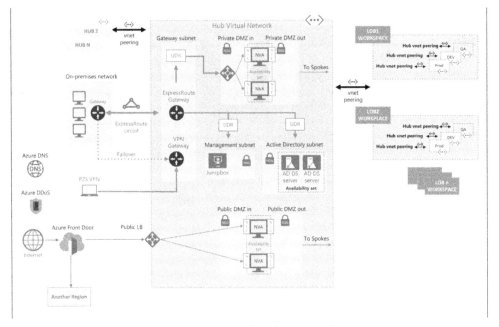

Figure 5.23 - Proposed Hub Network Setup

5.7 Resource Governance

To understand how to implement proper resource governance, let us see how resources are created in Azure. Before the *Azure Resource Manager* executes any resource management request, a set of controls are checked:

- Azure AD authenticates the request thought the trust relationship between a subscription that holds the resource in question and an Azure AD tenant.
- Azure RBAC authorizes the request.
- *Azure Policies* are evaluated (An Azure Policy can specify that users are only allowed to deploy a specific type of VM, for example).
- The request does not exceed an Azure subscription limit (e.g., maximum number of resource groups within a subscription).

- Financial commitment check is completed (verifies the subscription has enough payment information).
- Azure locks are evaluated.

We covered the authentication and authorization parts, and we talked about subscription limits. In this section, we will cover Azure Policies, Azure Locks, and cost management.

5.7.1 Azure Policies

Azure policies are a great way for ensuring Cloud governance. They can be assigned to management groups, subscriptions, and resource groups. When applied, it can have different effects (append, audit, deny, audit [if not exists], and deploy [if not exists]).

Another feature of Azure policies is the *policy initiatives*, a collection of policy definitions that serves the same goal. Instead of assigning individual Azure policies to resources, similar Azure policies can be put in a group (initiative), and that group of policies can be applied at a specific scope.

Even if you have one Azure policy, it is recommended to put it in an Azure policy initiative and assign the initiative instead of the individual policy. This makes your solution more flexible in case you need to add more policies with the same goal in the future. Here are some examples of Azure policy initiatives that you can apply in your virtual data center:

- **Azure Security Center Recommendations:** Applied to all management groups or the root management group and contains the following Azure policies:
  o Monitor unencrypted SQL database in Security Center (monitoring unencrypted SQL databases and servers).
  o Monitor missing system updates in Azure Security Center.
  o Monitor missing Endpoint Protection in Azure Security Center.

- **Restrict Public IP Creation:** Applied to all management groups or the root management group and contains one Azure policy:
  o Deny Public IP: prevents the creation of any new public IP endpoints

- **Data Encryption Recommendations:** Applied to all management groups or the root management group and contains one Azure policy:
  - o Enforce storage encryption: forces any storage account created to use encryption.

- **Geo-compliance and Data Sovereignty:** Applied to all management groups or the root management group and contains one Azure policy:
  - o Restrict allowed regions: restricts the creation of any resources to specific Azure regions.

- **Enforce Tags:** Applied to all management groups or the root management group and contains one Azure policy:
  - o Append a tag: append a tag if not defined.

- **Account Management:** Applied to all management groups or the root management group and contains the following Azure policies:
  - o Audit accounts with owner permissions who are not MFA-enabled on a subscription.
  - o Audit accounts with write permissions who are not MFA-enabled on a subscription.
  - o Audit external accounts with owner permissions on a subscription.
  - o Audit external accounts with write permissions on a subscription.
  - o Audit deprecated accounts on a subscription.

There are a lot of other policies that can be applied like *"Allowed virtual machine SKUs."* You should invest some time to see all available policies and apply the ones that match your security and governance needs.

5.7.2   Azure Locks

There are times when you need to lock a subscription, resource group, or resource to prevent users from accidently deleting or modifying critical resources. Azure locks can be used to restrict deletion (**CanNotDelete**) or modifying resources (**ReadOnly**).

Putting all VNET resources inside a resource group and applying a *(DoNotDelete)* Azure lock on the resource group level is a common practice. In another scenario, you might have periods where updates must not go into production. In these cases, the *(ReadOnly)* lock can be applied.

5.7.3   Cost Management

Cost management is a big topic by itself, but we will cover some tips that can help you effectively control the cost associated with your Cloud resources.

- Estimate the cost online using *Azure Pricing Calculator* before deploying resources.
- Add *tags* to your resources to group your billing data.
- Auto-shutdown VMs when not used.
- Use *Reserved Instances* when possible.
- Plan your VM sizes to avoid using high-end VMs when not needed.
- Turn on and check out *Azure Advisor* recommendations.

5.8   Deploy Services

Now that we have all preparation work completed, it is time to deploy resources. This is when your DevOps teams start to deploy resources in the already configured LOB workspaces that are configured with proper Azure RBAC models, Azure policies, and network security controls.

By using *Infrastructure as Code*, automation and continues integration and deployment pipelines, your DevOps teams can stay productive, and processes can be automated.

Since each *LOB workspace* is deployed as a separate subscription or subscriptions, DevOps teams have a lot of control over their environments. They get the agility Azure provides while ensuring compliance with the broader corporate security and isolation policies enforced through the *IT Shared Services* infrastructure.

5.8.1   Resource Groups

Each resource that you deploy in Azure is deployed inside a *resource group*. Resource groups serve as logical containers that can be used to assign policies, permissions, tags, and Azure locks. Azure policies, RBAC permissions, or locks assigned at the resource group level also apply to child resources. However, tags assigned at the resource group level don't propagate to child resources.

You can think of resource groups as the organizational units in Active Directory. Instead of assigning group policies and permissions to every object, you can group objects in organizational units and apply permissions and policies at the organizational unit level.

But resource groups are more than just containers. They represent a deployment scope so resources that share the same *life cycle* are grouped under one resource group. That way they can be provisioned together (e.g., via a template) and deleted together when the purpose of the resources does not exist anymore.

You should pause for a second and consider the effect of using Azure templates on the way you create resource groups. Whenever you generate an ARM automation script from the Azure portal, you always get the code for the entire resource group even if you're in the scope of a single resource. Therefore, it is important to keep resource groups narrower than broad.

Another approach is to combine all resources that comprise the specific deployment topology layer, like putting all shared services used by multiple applications in one resource group. For example, you can group all virtual network resources within a subscription into one resource group and then apply *CanNotDelete* Azure lock on the resource group level to prevent users from accidently deleting virtual networks.

Resource groups are also used to aggregate the cost associated with all child resources and scope spending to the resource group level.

5.8.2   Virtual Network Integration with PaaS

If you are considering using some PaaS services in Azure, like *Azure Storage* and *Azure SQL Database*, keep in mind that access to these services happens through the public internet. Your SecOps team might prefer to avoid using any service that relies on public endpoints for access and want this access to happen from within your Azure virtual networks. This can be due to a security policy that prevents internal workloads to access the public internet, which will also block access to such PaaS services. There are two patterns that can be used here to overcome this problem:

- **Use Virtual Network Service Endpoints.** This is an Azure feature that extends a virtual network's private address space and identity to Azure services over a direct connection. Service endpoints use the Microsoft backbone network and allow PaaS resources to be restricted to a single virtual network or inside a single subnet capable of using NSGs to further secure network access.
- **Deploy Azure services into virtual networks.** The PaaS service deploys dedicated instances into the virtual network, where only resources with access to that network can use them.

5.8.3   Management Roles

Earlier, we identified *SecOps, NetOps, SysOps, and DevOps* roles. The *LOB Workspace* SecOps and NetOps teams have the responsibility to lock down virtual networks and configure proper UDR routes to force traffic to be inspected by the central firewall in the *Hub Virtual Network*. They also have the responsibility of applying Azure policies to restrict creating public IPs and to restrict allowing certain SKUs of VMs, for example.

DevOps now have considerable flexibility in deploying resources in their environment. If they require internet or ExpressRoute access, the traffic goes through the central firewall in the *Hub Virtual Network*.

5.8.4   Service Model for Deployed Workloads

When DevOps teams decide to deploy a workload, they can decide for themselves whether they use SaaS, PaaS, or IaaS service models. This usually depends on the degree of trust over the Cloud platform and corporate needs and requirements. After all, the Azure platform offers a range of options to suit the level of control DevOps needs for workloads deployed to the virtual data center.

5.9   Security

Once you start deploying workloads in the Cloud and even after they are deployed, you should always consider security. Security management is a full-time job, and this is where your SecOps team can further lock down your virtual data center. In this section, we will cover key security services that can help you protect your Cloud resources and infrastructure.

5.9.1   Azure Key Vault

Securing your virtual data center is a top priority. All data must be encrypted at all times while in transit and at rest. But with encryption comes the overhead of managing and storing encryption keys. You should consider where encryption keys are stored and how they are rotated.

What you need is a key management service in the Cloud that can store and manage keys, secrets, and even certificates associated with encryption, authentication, and cryptographic operations.

Azure provides **Azure Key Vault** as the primary mechanism to manage encryption keys. Key Vault supports a *FIPS 140-2 Level 2-validated HSM* and allows you to generate keys using your on-premises HSM and securely transfer them to the Azure Key Vault.

You can use Azure Key Vault to encrypt storage assets and to help secure PaaS services or individual applications. For example, a *database connection string* can be stored in the Azure Key Vault instead of an application's configuration files or environment variables.

Within your virtual data center, you should deploy an Azure Key Vault per *LOB Application* or even per *LOB Environment* (production, dev, and QA).

5.9.2   Patch Management

Just because you are deploying VMs in the Cloud doesn't mean you stop patching them. If you are extending your on-premises network to the Cloud, you can use your on-premises patching infrastructure for patching Cloud VMs.

You can also configure your VMs to receive automatic updates from

Windows Update Services. This solution includes the *Update Management Solution* in Azure Automation to manage operating system updates for your Windows and Linux computers that are deployed in Azure.

5.9.3   DDoS

If you have published services in your virtual data center that are exposed to the public internet, then you should consider implementing a DDoS protection solution. Azure provides two tiers of protection against DDoS:

- **Basic Tier:** This is a free tier that is automatically enabled as part of the Azure platform. It provides real-time mitigation of common network-level attacks using the entire scale of Azure's global network.
- **Standard Tier:** This is a paid service that provides additional mitigation capabilities over the basic service tier that are tuned specifically to Azure virtual network resources. Policies are applied to public IP addresses associated to resources deployed in virtual networks. DDoS Protection Standard mitigates volumetric, protocol, and resource (application) layer attacks. When coupled with the Application Gateway web application firewall, DDoS Protection Standard can provide full layer 3 to layer 7 mitigation capability.

5.9.4   Malware Protection

For each VM you deploy, an anti-malware solution should be installed and configured. While you can extend your on-premises anti-malware solution to include your Cloud VMs, Azure provides free *anti-malware extension* for Windows VMs that you can also use. It is a free real-time protection capability that helps you identify and remove viruses, spyware, and other malicious software.

5.9.5   Azure Security Center

When you deploy resources in Azure and implement all security best practices, your job is far from being complete. Security is a never-ending job, and your security teams always have the responsibility of detecting threats and evaluating the overall security of your virtual data center.

But it becomes difficult to get a 360-degree view of your security estate in the Cloud with all different types of workloads. Therefore, you should consider using **Azure Security Center**, a great tool to manage all aspects of security in Azure. It can be described as a collection of best practices and recommendations brought together to help you strengthen your security posture.

Since it is offered as a native tool in Azure, it is deeply integrated with all Azure PaaS services and can detect and prevent threats in your virtual data center. By installing the Microsoft monitoring agent on Windows and Linux servers, Azure VMs are auto-provisioned in Azure Security Center.

5.9.6 Just-in-Time Virtual Machine Access

One of the most powerful security implementations in Azure is the *Just-in Time* VM access service (JIT VM access). If you have VMs with open management ports (e.g., SSH or RDP), then brute force attack can be used to gain access to your VMs, allowing an attacker to take control over your VMs and establish a foothold into your virtual data center.

To mitigate this risk, you can use JIT VM access to lock down inbound traffic to your Azure VMs. When users need access to a VM using a management port, they can submit a request. Only after validating the request using Azure RBAC permissions, the management ports are allowed, but only from the selected IP and port provided in the access request and only for a predefined period.

You should consider implementing JIT VM access to better lock management ports in your VMs, reducing by that your exposure to brute force attacks.

5.9.7 Encryption

Data encryption is important whether your data is hosted in the Cloud or on premises. You should enforce encryption for data in transit, data at rest, and data in use.

5.9.7.1 Data in Transit

Data should be encrypted when it moves between:

- your virtual data center and on-premises network either by using an encrypted *site-to-site* VPN or an isolated private ExpressRoute;
- workloads deployed in two virtual data centers;
- workloads deployed in the same virtual data center; or
- platform services, including internal and external endpoints.

You should spend time understanding all network traffic happening in your virtual data center and apply encryption to better protect your data.

5.9.7.2 Data at Rest

Data at rest should also be encrypted, including data stored on Azure *Storage Accounts* and in relational databases, which may offer additional encryption. For example, **Azure Storage Service Encryption** (**SSE**) provides encryption at rest for all Azure Storage services.

VM disk image encryption is also a critical part, especially in a shared tenant environment. You can use **Azure Disk Encryption** for VMs created in Azure, while you can *pre-encrypt* virtual machines on premises before migrating them to the Cloud.

5.9.7.3 Data in Process

Microsoft Azure supports **Confidential Computing**. It ensures that when data is "in the clear," which is required for efficient processing, the data is protected inside a trusted execution environment.

5.10 Monitoring, Alerts and Logging

Azure provides extensive monitoring, auditing, and logging features that helps you get verifiability and alerting from all component types. All teams should have access to such information for the resources they have access to. In this section, we will cover key monitoring and logging features offered by Azure.

5.10.1   Azure Monitor

Azure Monitor is a comprehensive solution for collecting, analyzing, and acting on telemetry from resources deployed in Azure. It helps you understand how your applications are performing and proactively identifies issues affecting them and the resources they depend on.

There are two major types of logs in Azure that you should consider:

- **Azure Activity Log** provides insight into the operations performed on resources in an Azure subscription.
- **Azure Monitor diagnostic logs** are generated by a resource and provide rich, frequent data about the operation of that resource.

It is also important to look at the Network Security Groups logs *(Event and Counter logs)* as they give you insights about allowed and denied traffic within your Cloud network infrastructure.

5.10.2   Log Archiving

But what about retaining logs? A good practice is to have all logs stored in encrypted Azure Storage accounts for audit, static analysis, or backup purpose. Such storage accounts are placed in the **IT Shared Audit and Monitor** subscription, and proper access management should be in place to restrict who can view or delete logs. Do not place the storage account used to store logs and the resource generating such logs in the same resource group. This way you can delete the resource group hosting that resource while retaining logs for compliant needs.

5.10.3   Operations Management Suite OMS

Another service that you can utilize in your virtual data center is the **Microsoft Operations Management Suite (OMS)**, which offers real-time operational insights through integrated search and custom dashboards that analyze all the records across all workloads in your virtual data center. Many OMS solutions can be included as a part of your virtual data center model, such as:

- **Anti-Malware Assessment**: This reports on malware, threats, and protection status.
- **Security and Audit:** The Security and Audit dashboard provides a high-level insight into the security state of resources by providing metrics on security domains, notable issues, detections, threat intelligence, and common security queries.
- **Change Tracking:** This solution allows customers to easily identify changes in the environment.

5.10.4 Azure Network Watcher

Azure Network Watcher provides you with network monitoring capabilities so you can visualize your network topologies and identify unhealthy connections and resources. It can be used to monitor, diagnose, view metrics, and enable or disable logs for resources in an Azure virtual network. It can also be used to check traffic flow from one location to another.

5.11   Business Continuity

Part of your reference architecture is planning for disasters. Bad things will always happen, and you want to be prepared by carefully planning your services and infrastructure. You can deploy failover connectivity to your on-premises network or choose to deploy two instances from the same service.

Just because you are hosting your workloads in the Cloud does not mean they are safe from failure of equipment or disruption from a platform patch deployed by the Cloud provider. In this section, we look at different options in Azure to ensure your services are available after different types of disruptions.

5.11.1 High Availability within an Azure Region

Within the same Azure region, you have two options to ensure availability for your VMs:

- **Availability Sets:** Putting two or more VMs in the same availability set ensures that at least one of the VMs hosted on Azure will be available if something happens within the same data center (different update and fault domains).
- **Availability Zones:** Putting two or more VMs in different availability zones ensure they are deployed in physically separate zones within an Azure region. Each availability zone will be distinct, possessing its own power, cooling, and high-speed, low-latency connections.

For example, when deploying two domain controllers in the hub virtual network, you can put them in their own availability set. The same applies to VMs in your data, business, and web tiers, as you can place VMs from the same tier in their own availability set.

5.11.2 Deploy Storage Redundancy

Storage redundancy should not be overlooked. Here are the storage redundancy options available in Azure:

- **Locally redundant storage (LRS):** Three copies of the data are maintained in a single region. LRS protects from normal hardware failures, but not from a complete failure of the region.
- **Zone-redundant storage (ZRS):** Three copies are maintained across three storage clusters (availability zone) in a single region.
- **Georedundant storage (GRS):** Six copies are maintained, three copies within the primary region and three copies in a secondary region. This provides the highest level of durability. In the event of a failure at the primary region, Azure Storage will fail over to the secondary region. Data in the secondary location is not available for write or read operations until Microsoft initiates a failover to the secondary region.

- **Read-access georedundant storage (RA-GRS):** This provides read-only access to the data replicated to the secondary location, even under normal conditions.

5.11.3 Deploying in Multiple Regions

Deploying applications in one Azure region means they are vulnerable to any outage that affects that region. To ensure high SLA, you can deploy the same project in two or more regions. This becomes handy when it comes to disaster recovery, ensuring global presence and diverting traffic between data centers.

When you plan to deploy workloads across two Azure regions, it is better to consider Azure-paired regions. Each Azure region is paired with another region within the same geography, together making a regional pair.

The reason behind this recommendation comes from the way Microsoft treats paired regions. Across region pairs, Microsoft will serialize platform updates so that only one paired region will be updated at a time. Furthermore, if there is an outage affecting multiple Azure regions, Microsoft will prioritize at least one region in each pair for recovery.

5.11.4 Recovery Services Vault

The Recovery Services Vault houses backup data and protects all configurations of Azure VMs in this architecture. With a Recovery Services Vault, you can restore files and folders from an IaaS VM without restoring the entire VM, enabling faster restore times.

5.12 Conclusion

In this chapter, we covered the CRA and identified the need for having one. Having a reference architecture when migrating workloads to the Cloud helps you ensure security, manageability, compliance, and consistency when deploying Cloud-based resources.

Remember that the goal for a successful Cloud migration project from deployment perspective is to maintain the balance between agility and governance. Developers are empowered to deploy services in the Cloud and meet their deadlines, while adhering to corporate security and compliance needs.

This calls for establishing a foundation architecture (enterprise scaffold) that guides your efforts when migrating to the Cloud. By taking the time to plan and configure your Cloud infrastructure and adopting key design patterns before deploying resources, you can have a smooth migration process without compromising security and governance.

6 Security

For a long time, security and compliance have been and still the main reasons that have slowed down Cloud adoption for many organizations. Businesses are concerned that moving to the Cloud might badly affect their security or make them uncompliant with different regulations and standards.

There is also a fear or a perception that putting sensitive information on the Cloud means they are available over the untrusted internet compared to being hosted behind on-premises corporate firewalls.

However, it is normal to have some sort of fear when you try something new, something that is assumed at first as untrusted. After all, moving to the Cloud means that your data and services are moving outside the control of your centralized IT teams, and this changes the way in which your organization gets services.

Such change is highly disruptive in nature as there is now a third party (Cloud provider) that is responsible for providing services on behalf of your organization, and there is a new shared trust model that evolves during this Cloud adoption journey.

In this chapter, we use the word *"customers"* to refer to organizations hosting workloads in the cloud, as they are customers to the Cloud provider.

6.1 Setting the Stage

Cloud means a lot of things depending on the person using it. SaaS is the most famous service model as it is easy to set up and consume, but IaaS is now gaining its momentum.

It goes without doubt that Cloud affects the cybersecurity practices in different ways due to different reasons. First, people who are migrating to the Cloud and spinning VMs and workloads usually do not have strong security knowledge, or security to them is not a top priority. They are usually focused on DevOps and the application side of the story, trying to get quick business benefits from consuming or migrating to the Cloud.

The second reason is that Cloud is *service-oriented* by nature, so organizations cannot interact directly with the physical infrastructure or deploy physical appliances to monitor what is going on inside that infrastructure. Organizations are relying on the Cloud provider giving them insights about what they think might be relevant to them. This is where a new shared trust model starts to evolve between organizations and the Cloud provider, which most organizations don't really understand. It gets lost in the translation.

In this section, we talk about how organizations think—and should think—about security and compliance in the Cloud. By doing so, we set the stage for the following sections as we dig deep into how security and compliance are different in the Cloud and how this requires a new security mind-set.

6.1.1 Attacks Happen in the Cloud

Just because you are migrating to the Cloud does not means attacks will not happen. Things like DDoS attacks and malware infections are common, even in the Cloud. In fact, Cloud computing tends to attract attackers as they are perceived to look as a huge collection of resources and data that are grouped into giant data centers.

Attacks on the Cloud can target the provider part of the Cloud stack and the customer's part. One example of attacks on the provider could be finding a vulnerability in the virtualization stack that might allow escaping the hypervisor and gaining access to other customer's resources due to the multitenancy nature of the cloud. Attacks on the customer part could be performing a vulnerability scan and finding unpatched operating systems, a misconfiguration, or weak passwords.

6.1.2 Due Diligence in Cloud Computing

Now that you know attacks can and will happen in a Cloud environment, you have a responsibility of evaluating the security of the Cloud provider you consider contracting with. This is part of your due diligence.

When it comes to Cloud migrations, due diligence is the process of evaluating Cloud providers to ensure that best practices are in place, such us verifying if there are adequate Cloud security controls that meet the level of service expected by your organization.

Most organizations jump into the Cloud and try to get business value from using the Cloud as soon as possible, without understanding the full scope of using Cloud computing first. Examples of things left undetermined are the incident response plan in the Cloud, the encryption use, and security monitoring. Not understanding these factors means you are taking on unknown levels of risks that you may not even comprehend.

To better align expectations between your organization and Cloud service providers, you should look at the contractual obligations for each party and understand how liability will be divided. Migrating to the Cloud affects governance, compliance, and security in big ways that should be considered early in the migration process. Therefore, there is a need for a new security mind-set to address all these variables.

6.1.3   The Need for a New Security Mind-set

As you are considering migrating to the Cloud or even in the process of such migration, you need to realize that the old way of doing security is no longer working anymore. Buying physical security appliances and plugging them into the network every time you face a security challenge is not going to work in the Cloud either. Not only you can't deploy physical appliances in the cloud, but the nature of Cloud computing and the velocity of changes in the Cloud makes it hard to carry on old practices of implementing isolated separately managed security solutions here and there.

Instead, a better way of carrying security practices to the Cloud is to think about security from a holistic standpoint and understand the limitations and benefits from operating in a Cloud environment. It requires taking advantage of the built-in security capabilities available in the Cloud platform and perhaps changing the way networks in the Cloud are separated to achieve best security scores.

It can be a great opportunity for you to rethink how you want to deliver various workloads and services with security in mind, using all the abstraction and orchestration capabilities that are not feasible otherwise on premises.

The questions that we answer in this chapter are *"How should you approach security and compliance in the Cloud?"*, *"Is the Cloud worth trusting?"*, and *"How is Cloud security different from traditional security measures used on premises?"*

6.1.4   Security Is Different in the Cloud

The most effective way to answer these questions is to understand Cloud security and compliance models and how they are different from the traditional way of doing security and compliance on premises. Only then, you can establish a security governance that can work for the Cloud, which helps you meet your compliance and legal requirements, thus creating the trust needed to migrate workloads to the Cloud.

Some organizations might think that migrating workloads to the Cloud is all what they need to worry about from a security and compliance perspective, as they assume the Cloud provides all the security measures needed to protect their data and workloads. This perception comes from the fact that many Cloud providers announce that they meet a broad set of international and industry-specific compliance standards, such as GDPR, ISO 27001, HIPAA, FedRAMP, SOC 1, and more.

While it is true that most Cloud providers meet many international and industry-specific compliance standards, there is much more to say here. The Cloud provider is responsible for the *security of the Cloud*; the customer is responsible for the *security in the Cloud*. According to a recent Gartner report, it is most likely that 95 percent of Cloud security failures will be the customer's fault. This is where the shared responsibility model comes to the picture.

6.2   The Shared Responsibility Model

Before digging into the shared responsibility model, it is essential to understand the Cloud computing stack as it will be used later to define the boundaries of the shared responsibility model. In this section, we define the Cloud computing stack and introduce the shared responsibility model for the Cloud's three service models.

6.2.1　Defining the Cloud Computing Stack

Cloud computing is essentially a shared pool of resources that are built with abstraction and orchestration in mind. Abstraction means that resources required to build the underlying physical infrastructure are abstracted into pools of resources waiting for you to use, while orchestration and automations are there to deliver set of resources from the pools to customers. This is what defines the Cloud.

Many organizations think that having a virtualization infrastructure means they operate a Private Cloud. But a key differentiator between the Cloud and traditional virtualization is the presence of the orchestration layer, which delivers resources on demand instead of relying on manual processes.

Cloud computing is also multitenant by nature, where multiple customers share the same pool of resources with strong isolation layer so they can only see and modify their assets and data, not other customer assets or data.

To demonstrate the concept of the shared responsibility model, it is better to look at the Cloud as a stack of resources. At the foundation of the stack, there are physical facilities and servers. On top of that are the virtualization layer (abstraction layer), the core connectivity and networking stack, and the computing stack.

All these resources are exposed using management and orchestration APIs that customers use to manage various Cloud resources, such as launching a VM. Those APIs are called the *"cloud management plane"*, and this is what customers usually use to remotely manage resources. Up till now, this part of the stack is what defines the IaaS service model.

On top of the previously mentioned resources, there is the middleware and integration layer, which can be in the form of functions such as database and queuing or application development platform. This part of the stack is what defines the PaaS service model. This layer is built on top of the IaaS part of the stack, and the customer only sees the platform, not the underlying infrastructure.

Finally, SaaS services are often seen as an application layer and data storage that is exposed via an API and a presentation layer (web browser or mobile applications). Most modern Cloud applications use a combination of IaaS and PaaS services.

6.2.2 Scope and Responsibilities

When you migrate to the Cloud, your security team is responsible for the same things, just in the Cloud. Moving to the Cloud does not mean the same on-premises security domains and practices used for decades now are no longer relevant. What is changed is the roles and responsibilities, along with the implementation of controls.

Moreover, the nature of risk is dramatically changed in the Cloud. There is a new party (Cloud provider) that is now responsible for hosting your data and resources. Therefore, security responsibilities are now distributed across the Cloud stack and the parties involved (your organization and the Cloud provider).

This is known as the shared responsibility model, as shown in figure 6.1, which is a responsibility matrix that depends on the service model (IaaS, PaaS, SaaS), deployment model (Public, Private, Community, Hybrid), and the feature or product. It also depends on the Cloud provider and the list of security controls they offer.

It might be a good way to look at the shared responsibility model as a function of the degree of control each party (customer and Cloud provider) has over the cloud stack. The more control each party has over the stack, the more responsible he is.

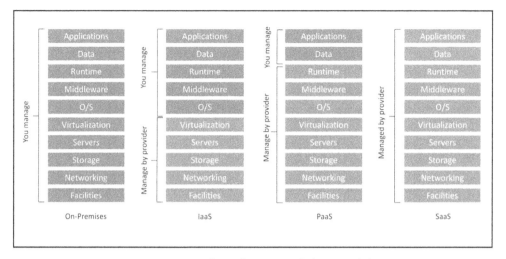

Figure 6.1 - Shared Responsibility Model

6.2.2.1 Software as a Service

With SaaS, the degree of control that customers have is so small. They cannot access the underlying infrastructure that the service is running on top of, and they are only presented usually with a visualization layer accessible via a browser, a mobile app, or an API. Since customers cannot alter how the application works, then the Cloud provider is responsible for nearly all security.

A good example could be using Salesforce, a well-known CRM solution offered as a SaaS-based service. The Cloud provider in this case is responsible for the physical security of the infrastructure, host patching, and application security. On the other hand, the customer is responsible only for managing their use of the application and configuring authorizations and entitlements.

6.2.2.2 Platform as a Service

It is usually hard for customers to envision the shared responsibility model for the PaaS, due to the broad set of Cloud offerings that fits under this service model. Nevertheless, it can be put in simple words. The Cloud provider is responsible for securing the platform, while customers are responsible for their implementation on the platform, including how they configure security features.

When using *Database as a Service*, the provider is responsible for the infrastructure and host patching, while the customer is responsible for turning on database security features, managing accounts and authentication. It can be said that with PaaS, the responsibilities are evenly split.

6.2.2.3 Infrastructure as a Service

This is where the customer is responsible for more things than the provider. The Cloud provider is responsible for everything up to the virtualization layer over the Cloud stack, while customers are responsible for everything they build on that infrastructure. For example, the customer is fully responsible for securing the operating system of VMs, logically segmenting the network, and monitoring their infrastructure for attacks.

6.2.3 Defense in Depth in the Cloud

The famous defense in-depth technique still applies to the Cloud, but with the shared responsibility model in mind. The end goal is to provide protection for the infrastructure, applications, and data, as shown in figure 6.2.

Cloud providers have huge resources put together to ensure the security of their services, and they are very good at doing that, while customers are constrained with IT budgets when it comes to protecting assets on premises.

But keep in mind that with the shared responsibility model, Cloud providers are very good in securing only the areas they are responsible for. They are not going to look at the areas they are not responsible for, although they might provide you tools to help you figure out your security maturity level in the areas you are responsible for.

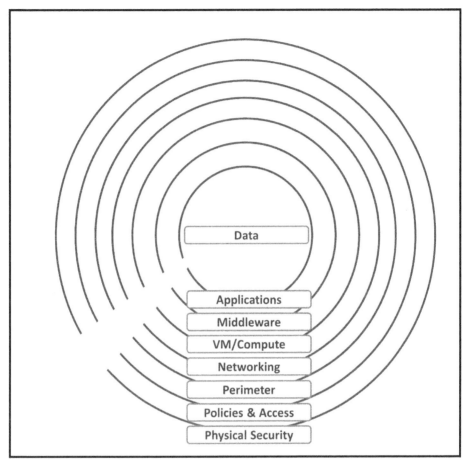

Figure 6.2 - Defense In Depth

Cloud providers provide foundation services like the facility, hardware, and virtualization layer (hypervisor). These are things that they are going to take a lot of responsibility for as they don't allow you to access and patch the hypervisor, for example. Instead they are going to do it for you.

The physical security for data centers is another good example of what the Cloud provider is responsible for. Things like guards, physical access to the data center, and any additional facilities, including generators, UPS systems, air-conditioning, and fire-suppression systems. Cloud providers take full responsibility for all that, and they are good at it.

Most of the foundational services in the Cloud stack is the Cloud provider's responsibility, and due to their foundational nature, these services do not provide tangible value to the business. This is where customers start to come on top and where the shared responsibility model comes in.

Take networks, for example. Cloud providers allow you to logically separate networks by creating different subnets and virtual networks, but they are not going to inspect the traffic flowing inside a subnet or between subnets, as this is your responsibility. If you are allowing insecure ports into your Cloud networks, then it is your responsibility to start looking and understanding the threats coming in.

The same applies to VMs. The provider offers a shared pool of resources and a virtualization layer to help you quickly create VMs. While the provider is responsible for securing the virtualization stack and patching it, the operating system running inside VMs is your responsibility. In other words, the provider is not going to patch and manage the operating system for you. Cloud providers simply do not know the admin account for the operating system, and they cannot manage it or log in. Therefore, they are not responsible for it.

If you decide to install an old version of Windows on a VM without any patches and you make it accessible over the internet, then it is your responsibility if that machine gets hacked. It makes sense after all.

You are also responsible for a lot of things like access management, the choice of ports and protocols being used, configuration management, and more. One of the essential things you are responsible for is looking at logs. This is not a new thing as you have been looking at logs for years. Just because you moved to the Cloud does not mean you stop doing that.

When it comes to applications deployed into the Cloud, most of it is your responsibility. You are responsible for writing a secure code, using encrypted communications, and hosting the application in a secure underlying infrastructure. This is almost the same if you would host the application on premises. Just because it is hosted in the Cloud does not mean you disregard all the security best practices known for years.

6.3 How Security Is Different with Cloud Networking

It is common to see customers mapping their exact network topology they have on premises to the Cloud. If you maintain a DMZ and an internal-protected network inside your data center, you would create a replica of the two subnets in your Cloud tenant. This is usually a common practice, especially in shift-and-lift migration cases.

While this might work for you, it might not be the optimal implementation for network security. Remember that the Cloud is a different playground and you should plan your network topology in the Cloud with security in mind, acknowledging the shared responsibility model and the nature of the Cloud stack.

With Cloud computing, things are different. There is no direct management access for customers to the underlying physical network. Well, what does this mean? One example how this can affect network security is the inability for network intrusion detection systems (that are based on mirroring traffic) to have access to the host network traffic for inspection. The workaround would be implementing *in-line* virtual appliances or software agents in instances. This might introduce an increase in processing and might slow down your network.

In this section, we talk about what is different in Cloud networking so you can plan your network security when migrating to the Cloud. We start by introducing *software-defined networks* and how they can be used to create layers of isolation. We also cover other concepts like *virtual appliances*, the *hybrid Cloud connection*, and *immutable workloads*.

6.3.1 Software-Defined Networks (SDNs)

Software-defined networks or SDNs are a great capability that can be described as introducing an abstraction layer on top of the networking hardware. This means that the network control plan is isolated from the data plan (decoupling). It opens the door for overcoming many traditional limitations of a LAN and enables new types of security controls as illustrated next.

6.3.1.1 New Isolation Layer

One of the direct benefits of SDNs is the ability to quickly and easily create as many isolated networks as needed, thanks to the abstraction layer. This means it is easier now to create many isolated security zones by separating them into different subnets or virtual networks and applying security controls and firewalls to inspect and restrict data flow passing in between. In fact, you can even assign the same IP address range to two different subnets to prevent any communication between them due to addressing conflict.

6.3.1.2 What Is Wrong with Traditional Firewalls?

SDNs give you the ability to do things (in software) in a layer that's decoupled from the underlying hardware. This means you can define things in software (via a template or policy) and the Cloud orchestration layer can build or apply the changes defined in software.

One of the new ways the Cloud affects networking is the ability to define policies and templates in software and the rise of SDNs. Traditionally, you use VLANs to separate different types of workloads according to their criticality and access requirements. A firewall could be implemented so that traffic between VLANs is inspected and monitored.

With Cloud computing and the elasticity nature of the Cloud, customers tend to break down a complicated workload that was hosted on one VM to different components that are hosted in different VMs so that they can scale independently. This means that workloads moving to the Cloud are usually spread out into more specialized workloads that have different scaling and availability requirements.

From a networking perspective, in order to logically separate these workloads to facilitate applying firewall access rules on the subnet level, each workload is put into a different subnet, and a firewall is placed to intercept traffic between different subnets. The problem with this approach is that with the increased number of subnets, it becomes difficult to manage firewall rules and control the traffic between Cloud subnets.

Furthermore, firewalls placed at the edge of the subnet can only intercept traffic flowing between subnets and not within. This might introduce the risk of an attacker moving laterally between VMs within the same subnet. Moving to a host-level firewall can solve this problem, but it comes with two issues:

1. They are hard to manage at scale.
2. If the system they are running on is compromised, they are easy to disable.

One proposed solution is to use *micro-segmentation*, which is introduced in the next section.

6.3.1.3 The Power of Micro-Segmentation

The revolution happening in the SDNs area allows for a new way to protect assets. Instead of having edge firewalls protecting traffic going in and out of a subnet, SDN firewalls can apply to the assets themselves based on some more flexible criteria (like tagging).

SDN firewalls are a set of policies that defines *egress* and *ingress* rules that can apply to a single asset (VM) or group of assets (e.g., based on a tag), regardless of the network location (within a virtual network).

Why is this so powerful? An example can demonstrate the power of such software-defined firewalls. VMs in an auto-scale group are automatically deployed in multiple subnets with a load balancer in front to distribute the load. Then you can create a firewall ruleset that applies to these instances, regardless of their IP address or subnet. This is a powerful approach for securing Cloud networks that use different architecture than traditional networks.

6.3.2 Security with Virtual Appliances

While micro-segmentation is a great way to protect and inspect traffic between different subnets and virtual networks, you still might need a specialized application firewall (operating at layer 7) to further inspect traffic within your Cloud infrastructure.

Since you cannot onboard your physical appliances to the Cloud, virtual appliances become a possible solution only if needed and with a proper routing and network segmentation. The concern here is that virtual appliances deployed in the Cloud that are used for network monitoring should play by the Cloud's new rules, or else they might not be the optimal solution.

There are a couple of challenges that you should be aware of during your Cloud migration when it comes to deploying virtual appliances in the Cloud. First, since virtual appliances used to inspect network traffic might be installed *in-line* or at the instance level, they might introduce increase of the processing on the instance itself, or they might be a bottleneck slowing down the network.

It is also important to consider the elasticity nature of the Cloud. If a virtual appliance is deployed to protect a web application deployed in a scale set, then depending on the amount of traffic coming to the web application, that web application might scale out to handle the traffic, and if the traffic is high, another web application instance might be activated in different locations to balance the traffic. This means that when deploying virtual appliances, they should support such elasticity of the Cloud resources they protect.

Another important aspect of the Cloud is that the velocity of change is higher than that of physical networks, and virtual appliances need to take this into consideration. For example, it is normal in Cloud environments that the lifetime of a virtual server has a short lifetime. The question is, "How could this affect virtual appliances?"

Virtual appliances tend to operate in a fixed environment or, at least, where changes are minimal. They used to identify resources by their IP address since most key resources are assigned fixed IP addresses or a network name.

In the Cloud, however, the life span of servers can be less than an hour in case of a scale set for example. In such environment, IP addresses will change far more quickly than on traditional networks, which security tools must account for. Ideally, network assets should be identified by a unique ID or tags, not an IP address or a network name.

Furthermore, IP addresses are most likely assigned dynamically in the Cloud, and even if they are assigned statically, different resources may share the same IP over a short period of time. This means that alerts triggered by network monitoring tools that use the IP address to identify a resource should be adjusted accordingly. Moreover, when investigating a suspicious behavior in the network during an incident response life cycle, you should take this into consideration as well.

6.3.3 Hybrid Cloud Connection

Before migrating to the Cloud, you might need to create a secure connection from your private network to your Cloud tenant to route traffic and migrate data or workloads. Therefore, it is highly preferable if the private address range used in your Cloud networks don't overlap with the private address assignment on premises.

The key thing to remember is that this connection might affect and reduce the security of the Cloud network, if your on-premises private network isn't at an equivalent security level. Attackers can compromise your on-premises infrastructure (employee's laptop) and then use that to scan the entire Cloud deployment and move laterally to the Cloud network via the hybrid Cloud connection.

One solution to prevent the propagation of attacks to move from the private network to the Cloud via the hybrid connection is to enforce an access control and deploy a firewall to control the traffic moving between both environments. This calls for a *hub-and-spoke* network model in the Cloud where the *hub* hosts security controls for all traffic passing from your on-premises network to your Cloud virtual networks.

Hybrid Cloud connections are not needed in all cases, and if they are, it is highly recommended to minimize the number of the hybrid Cloud connections for security and management reasons.

One preferred and flexible architecture for a hybrid Cloud connectivity is the *"Bastion Virtual Network,"* as shown in figure 6.3. In this architecture, it is possible to connect multiple Cloud networks to your on-premises data center via one hybrid Cloud connection. You build a dedicated virtual network for the hybrid connection and then peers any other networks through the designated bastion network. You can also deploy firewall rulesets to protect traffic flowing in and out of the hybrid connection.

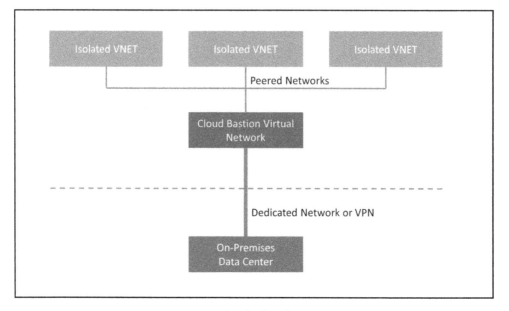

Figure 6.3 - Hybrid Cloud Connectivity

6.3.4   The Rise of Immutable Workloads

While VMs are full abstraction of operating systems, containers are the next level of abstraction. They are code execution environments within the operating system, sharing the same operating system and kernel. Therefore, multiple containers can run on the same VM, and they are known for launching incredibly rapidly since they don't need to boot an operating system.

A very interesting implementation of containers is when they are used in the Cloud with auto-scaling and when they are launched dynamically based on an image. In such a scenario, instances can be turned off when no longer needed without affecting the application stack.

This also implies that instances are immutable to changes. Each time they are instantiated, they are launched from the same image, which means that any changes happening while they are running will not persist. Therefore, they are called immutable workloads.

So how this is related to security? Immutable workloads enable significant security features:

- Since instances are launched based on an image, patching the image ensures the newly instantiated instances are running the patched version always, which eliminates the need to patch a running workload. Instead of patching an image, replacing the image with a new gold master image can be another good approach, which means you don't need to worry about broken patches anymore.
- Remote logins to running workloads can be disabled to prevent changes that will not persist after shutdown.
- Rolling a new version is easier now since all what you need is to update the master image.
- It is easier to disable services and whitelist applications and processes since the instance should never change.
- Vulnerability assessment can be performed during image creation.

6.4   Data Protection in the Cloud

We are living in times where cyberattacks make the headlines and cost billions of losses for businesses all around the world. In fact, Matt Nelson, president and CEO of AvaLAN Wireless, warns that the United States' next Pearl Harbor will be cyberattack. A range of highly publicized data leaks in recent years have resulted in financial loss, legal repercussions, resignation of top executives, and damaged brand reputation.

Data breaches happen all the time whether the data is hosted on premises or in the Cloud. However, the organization hosting its data in the Cloud is the one that owns the data (data owner) and is the one responsible when such breaches occur, even if the cause of the data breach lies with the Cloud-hosting organization.

Moreover, if such breach is publicized, the negative attention will be focused more on the data owner more than on the Cloud provider. Therefore, the *Cloud Security Alliance* recommends that sensitive data should be encrypted with approved algorithms and long random keys.

Encryption is so important for industries that need to meet regulatory compliance requirements. Combined with other security measures, encryption enables organizations to meet the stringent compliance requirements of HIPAA (for health-care organizations and business associates), PCI DSS (for e-commerce and retail organizations), and SOX (for financial reporting). This is because encrypted data can only be read by authorized parties with access to the decryption keys. Even if the data falls into the wrong hands, it is useless if its keys remain secure. This is especially beneficial when data is migrated and hosted in the Cloud as it protects data content if a provider, account, or system is compromised.

Clearly, there is a risk in moving data from a presumably secure data center into the hands of a Cloud provider, whether the data is migrated to a SaaS or IaaS. While it is common that a risk assessment is conducted to identify what sensitive data needs to be encrypted, many organizations default to encrypting all data that gets migrated to the Cloud.

6.4.1 How to Do It Right

Data protection can be achieved by different means and technologies like encryption and access controls. While there are many things to consider when dealing with data protection in the Cloud, here are some major areas to focus on:

- Choosing a secure protocol always (TLS over SSL, SSH over Telnet).
- Encrypting and protecting data in-transit and at-rest.
- Using effective encryption technologies (key rotation and key management).
- Maximizing access controls for sensitive data.
- Using auditing and reporting functionality.
- Adhering to corporate and industry compliance policies.

6.4.2 What Types of Data Require Cloud Encryption?

The following types of data are especially susceptible and should always be encrypted by enterprises and organizations that store it:

- **Financial data:** Any kind of financial data, such as credit card information, bank account numbers, and credit-related information, must be protected. Throughout the world, PCI DSS regulations require strict security measures for any company that deals with credit cards.

- **Public company accounting:** For publicly traded companies, the Sarbanes-Oxley rules regulate the reporting of financial data by public companies and require auditable security measures.
- **Health data:** Information about health insurance, medical care, and personal data like social security numbers or home addresses must be kept private. US guidelines for this type of data are mandated in the HIPAA regulations.
- **Sensitive Security Information (SSI):** This includes confidential business materials such as internal research and development documents or IT vulnerability assessment reports.
- **Personally Identifiable Information (PII):** This is any information that pertains to an individual, including names, addresses, and social security numbers.
- **IT Systems Security Information:** This information makes up the technology infrastructure of a company, such as encryption keys, certificates, passwords, and Cloud service access credentials.

Also falling under this are the following:

- **Government data:** All US governmental agencies are required to follow FISMA guidelines to protect data from security breaches. Information about government programs falls under these regulations.
- **Military data:** This is, of course, a part of the government, but with its own unique and even more stringent requirements.

6.4.3 Securing Cloud Data Transfers

Once the *what-to-encrypt data* has been identified, the next thing to discuss is when and how to encrypt data. You should always protect data when it is migrated to the Cloud, and once migrated, it should be protected at rest.

6.4.3.1 Encrypt Data Before Uploading to The Cloud

Before migrating content to the Cloud, you should take time to understand the provider's data migration mechanisms because leveraging provider mechanisms is often more secure and cost-effective than manual methods such as secure file transfer protocol (SFTP).

When migrating content to the Cloud, there are two options to encrypt the data in-transit depending on what the Cloud provider and platform support is. Network encryption is relying on the communication channel to be encrypted, like using TLS or SFTP. And client-side encryption is encrypting data before migrating to the Cloud.

When migrating to SaaS, it is important that any link used to transfer information is secured using TLS or a similar secure protocol. For example, there are many third-party tools out there that can help migrating documents from file servers to SharePoint Online. It is recommended to look at the encryption capabilities and protocols each tool is using before making a choice to use one.

Migrating other types of workloads is also challenging, like migrating VMs and databases. For VM migration, the Cloud provider might have solutions to offer, and there are third-party tools that can migrate VMs. A site-to-site VPN might be required to securely migrate such workloads to the Cloud.

However, if the tool being used to migrate workloads does not support encryption or it supports in-sufficient encryption, the data should be encrypted by a third party before migrating to the Cloud (client-side encryption), and then encryption can be reversed after the migration is completed. For example, if you are uploading documents from a file server to a Cloud storage that only supports insecure HTTP API calls, then encrypting documents using a third-party encryption tool before migration is a good practice.

6.4.3.2 Use Secure Protocols to Connect

After migrating data to the Cloud or even during such migration, it is important to always connect to Cloud resources (especially the management plan) using a secure protocol. Establishing a site-to-site VPN or client VPN to the Cloud provider's network is a good way to protect any data communication between your corporate network and Cloud resources.

However, it is common to see VMs assigned public IP addresses and being accessible using remote management protocols such as remote desktop protocol (RDP). While this might be necessary in some situations, it is recommended to restrict what IP addresses can connect to these machines to reduce the surface attack.

Some organizations usually create a dedicated subnet in the Cloud to act as a staging area before connecting to other Cloud resources. If the Cloud administrator needs to perform any administrative task, he first connects to a server (*bastion workstation* or *jumpbox*) deployed in that subnet after performing two-factor authentication to prove his identity and then jumping to other Cloud resources.

Other organizations put more restricted rules before allowing a remote administration tasks to happen in the Cloud, like requiring a compliant machine (patch level or updated antivirus software) or domain-joined workstation.

6.4.4   Securing Data at Rest

Now that we have covered securing data transfer to the Cloud, how can you protect data at rest? Access controls and encryption are used for this purpose, as discussed next.

6.4.4.1 Access Controls

Cloud data protection can be achieved by defining data access controls in different levels, like restricting access to the Cloud management plane and application level controls. An entitlement matrix can list which users, groups, and roles should access which resources and functions. Using Role-based access control (RBAC) is a common way to define roles and manage access to Cloud resources by assigning people to roles. Each role is assigned or granted a set of actions and privileges. Most Cloud providers allow you to define your own custom roles if the built-in roles do not fit your access management needs.

6.4.4.2 Encryption and Tokenization

The risk of having unencrypted data at rest is high as attackers can gain access to the storage and compromise it. In a recent attack, a cache of more than sixty thousand files were discovered on a publicly accessible Amazon server, including passwords to a US government system containing sensitive information and at least a half-dozen unencrypted passwords belonging to government contractors with top-secret facility clearance. This is how badly things can escalate without proper data protection controls.

Depending on the workload and Cloud service being used, different encryption techniques can be used to protect data in rest. This can be VM disks, blob storage, or even database files. Most Cloud providers offer encryption capabilities in their platform that are turned on by default or require customers to turn it on. An example would be database encryption offered by the platform to encrypt databases like *Transparent Database Encryption (TDE)*.

Another option to protect data at rest is known as *tokenization*, which is often used when the format of the data is important (like replacing credit card numbers in an existing system that requires the same format text string). Tokenization takes the data, replaces it with a random value, and then stores the original and the randomized version in a secure database for later recovery.

6.4.5   Key Management in the Cloud

Once the data is encrypted, you should ask yourself, "who owns and manages the encryption keys?". This question helps you understand who can decrypt and access your encrypted data in the Cloud. If you are using the built-in encryption capabilities of the provider, then most likely (but not necessarily) the Cloud provider is the one who manages the encryption keys and thus can decrypt the data. This scenario has its own advantages as it is easier for you to use the built-in encryption capabilities of the platform, compared to the complexity of onboarding third-party tools. However, depending on the Cloud service being used, there might be an option for you to onboard your own encryption keys or *Bring Your Own Key (BYOK)*.

When it comes to key management, the main deciding factor is performance, latency, and security. That is, can the encryption key be retrieved to the right service at the right time while maintaining high levels of security and compliance requirement? There are a lot of options available to you here.

- **Use Hardware Security Module (HSM).** You can use your already deployed HSM devices on premises to deliver keys to the Cloud over a secure connection or use an HSM device provided by the Cloud provider.
- **Use a Cloud provider service.** Most Cloud providers have a key management system that is available to customers and are deeply integrated within their services and platform. For example, Microsoft offers *Azure Key Vault* as a key management services, while *Key Management Service (KMS)* is available in AWS.
- **Use hybrid.** A combination of both approaches can be used for different workloads depending on the type and sensitivity of data.

6.5   Identity and Access Management in the Cloud

One of the critical aspects of moving to the Cloud is to figure out how to properly deal with identity and access management (IAM). Understanding what needs to change in identity management is one of the first things to consider for any Cloud migration project. There are two main concerns when dealing with IAM in the Cloud:

- For years now, organizations are using NTLM and Kerberos as the main authentication protocols in their on-premises networks. The problem is that these protocols are not built or designed for the Cloud.
- There is the complexity of managing identities across different systems on premises and in the Cloud, for example, the need to provision the same user on different systems on premises and in the Cloud.

To address the first point, you should look at different forms of authentication and authorization technologies that can work in the Cloud, while federation helps building the trust between on-premises systems and Cloud services, reducing the complexity of managing identities (second point).

Essentially migration to Cloud is a golden opportunity to build a new infrastructure on modern architecture and standards. In fact, migrating to the Cloud can be a forcing function for organizations to confront their identity and access practices and update them to deal with the differences in the Cloud.

6.5.1   IAM Standards for Cloud Computing

The following are most common IAM standards that are supported by most Cloud providers:

- **Security Assertion Markup Language (SAML) 2.0**: this standard supports both authentication and authorization. It uses XML to make an association between an identity provider and a relaying party.
- **OAuth**: this standard is used for authorization and is widely used for web services.
- **OpenID:** this standard is very widely supported for web services.

Let us see how SAML can be used to enable single sign-on (SSO) for Cloud applications. SAML is an XML-based open standard that eliminates the need for multiple application-specific user names and passwords. SAML authentication requires three entities:

- The user trying to access a service
- A service provider (SP), the application providing the service (e.g., Office 365 or Salesforce)
- An identity provider (IdP), the application authenticating the user (e.g., Microsoft Federation Services or Azure Active Directory)

Figure 6.4 shows how SAML SSO flow works:

- A user begins by attempting to access the Cloud application (SP).
- The Cloud application generates a SAML authentication request and redirects the user to the *IdP* for authentication.
- The *IdP* verifies whether the user is authenticated or not. If not, the user is asked to enter his authentication details.
- Once successfully authenticated, the *IdP* generates a SAML response.

- Now the *IdP* redirects the user back to the *SP*, along with the SAML response.
- The *SP* validates the SAML response and grants the user access.

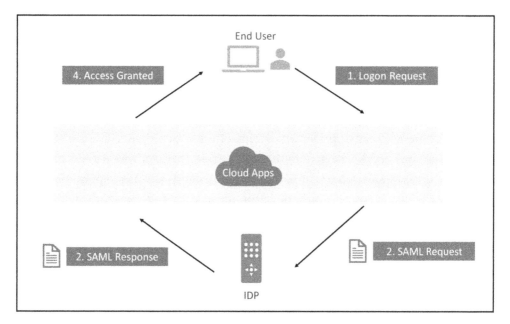

Figure 6.4 - SAML SSO Flow

6.5.2   Manage Identities in the Cloud

To start this process, there should be a discussion between the organization and the Cloud provider on how identities should be managed. This discussion will help the organization understand what the identity management capabilities that the Cloud provider supports are to plan how to move forward with identities in the Cloud.

At a minimum, the Cloud provider should support internal identities and attributes for users accessing the Cloud service and support federation, so organizations do not have to manually create identities in the Cloud and have separate sets of credentials. This gives organizations a clear idea about the options available before planning which approach to use.

For a user to access Cloud resources, there should be a user object in the Cloud identity system that represents that user with some attributes, and there must be a way for the Cloud identity system to authenticate the session before granting access. Here are two common ways to do that:

- Organizations can manually provision and manage users in the Cloud system in separation of the on-premises identity system and issue each one a separate set of credentials. However, this is not scalable for most organizations.
- Organizations can synchronize on-premises identities with the Cloud identity system and configure federation to facilitate SSO.

There are many options and architectural models when it comes to IAM in the Cloud. The goal should be to enable organizations to extend their identity systems to support authentication to any SaaS application and enforce stronger authentication protocols and methods while reducing the management cost and enhancing security. If you are going to use Salesforce, for example, how can users log on and authenticate with the same set of credentials they use on premises, without the need to manually provision all users in Salesforce?

A good design should also scale well. Today it is Salesforce, but tomorrow there might be other Cloud services that need authentication. There are famous *identity as a service* providers out there that can significantly help with this. One of them is *Microsoft Azure Active Directory*, which acts as a Cloud-based identity management system that can help organizations sync their identities to the Cloud (Azure Active Directory) and enable SSO with thousands of SaaS applications with minimal effort. It can also enforce strong authentication methods like MFA and require a compliant device before authenticating.

6.5.3 Secure Identities in the Cloud

Now that you know different options to manage and extend your identities to the Cloud, the next thing you should look at is how to secure these identities. There are a lot of options we discuss next, like Multi-factor authentication (MFA) and *Attribute-Based Access Control*, but there are more. Anomaly detection is now a common way to identify risky sessions and detect compromised credentials.

6.5.3.1 Multi-Factor Authentication (MFA)

MFA is one of the strongest options for reducing account takeovers. It helps you mitigate the risks from using weak passwords and comprised credentials that can lead to data breaches and loss of data. Relying on a single factor (a password) for Cloud services is very high risk. There are multiple options for MFA, including:

- **Hard tokens:** physical devices that generate one-time passwords.
- **Soft tokens:** an application that runs on a phone or computer.
- **Biometrics:** the use of biometric readers, which are commonly available.

6.5.3.2 Attribute-Based Access Control (ABAC)

Another way to protect resources in the Cloud is by using Attribute-Based Access Control (ABAC), which is also known as *policy-based access controls*. Unlike RBAC, ABAC policies can use any type of attribute (user attributes, resources attributes, environment attribute, etc.).

Microsoft Azure Active Directory provides a service called Conditional Access that can evaluate and restrict access depending on some environmental attributes. Here are some questions Azure Active Directory conditional access can anticipate:

- Is the user coming from a compliant device?
- Is the user connecting from a domain-joined device?
- Is the user connecting from a trusted network?
- Is the user using an approved client app?
- Is the user's session risky (coming from a tor browser or risky IP)?

6.6   Compliance

So far, we've talked about security in the Cloud. But what about ensuring compliance in the Cloud? How is compliance in the Cloud different? And how do we enforce compliance in the Cloud?

The Cloud affects the way organizations deliver and measure

compliance. It goes without saying that compliance is one of the major reasons many organizations hesitate to fully adopt a Cloud-first strategy. However, a clear understanding of how compliance is achieved in the Cloud enables organizations to capitalize on the business agility that the Public Cloud promises.

It can be challenging to show auditors that your organization is in compliant when using Cloud computing. Because of the importance of compliance as a tool for governance and risk management, understanding the implication of Cloud on compliance is a key component of any Cloud strategy.

When talking about compliance, audits are usually involved. However, there is more to compliance than audits and more to audits than using them to ensure regulatory compliance. They are so related topics, and both are important when discussing Cloud migrations. But what does compliance mean? And how does it relate to audits?

Compliance can be thought of as a way to validate awareness of and adherence to corporate obligations such as laws, regulations, and contracts. Such regulations can also be in the form of corporate social responsibilities, ethics, strategies, and policies. Not only is compliance concerned with assessing the state of that awareness and adherence, it is also about assessing the risk and potential cost of noncompliance against the cost to achieve compliance. This helps organizations prioritize, fund, and initiate any corrective actions deemed necessary.

Audits, on the other hand, are a key tool for proving or disproving compliance. Audits, compliance, and governance are all related topics, and they are highly affected when operating in a Cloud environment.

6.6.1   Compliance as a Shared Responsibility

The same shared responsibility model that applies to security also applies to compliance. Compliance is a shared responsibility in the Cloud. Therefore, it is wrong to assume that once data and workloads are migrated to the Cloud, then the compliance responsibility shifts entirely to the Cloud provider.

The higher up the Cloud stack an organization buys into, the more security and compliance functionality is built-in by the cloud provider. In the case of SaaS application, for instance, the application provider offers a variety of additional security and compliance features that are built into the product. But since this is a shared responsibility, it is the customer's responsibility to implement and use these security and compliance features.

6.6.2   Who Is Responsible for Compliance?

It is also important to keep in mind that customers are always ultimately responsible for their own compliance, even if compliance is a shared responsibility between customers and the Cloud provider, and they must always remain in control.

If we look at the *Data Protection Act* in the UK, it clearly states that the data controllers (the organization using the Cloud) should be in control of data at any given stage, even if the data is sent to an external party.

Let's look at an example. If an organization is trying to comply with an internal policy or a regulation, then it is responsible to do whatever it takes to achieve that. It can choose to keep its data on premises and apply all measures necessary to comply like encrypting data, defining access rules, and managing other controls. If it decides to migrate data to the Cloud, then it is responsible for evaluating Cloud providers and being aware of the type of Cloud services it uses.

Ensuring compliance in the Cloud starts with evaluating Cloud providers. During the Cloud provider evaluation process, organizations must understand their compliance alignment and gaps, and in the world of Public Clouds, this is achieved by relying more on third-party attestations of the Cloud provider. This is because Public Cloud providers do not allow organizations to perform their own audits on their services.

Instead, Public Cloud providers engage with third-party firms to perform audits and issue attestations that organizations can then use to evaluate if the service meets their compliance obligations. Usually many Cloud providers are certified for various regulations and industry requirements, such as PCI DSS, SOC1, SOC2, HIPPA, and even global/ regional regulations like the EUGDPR.

6.6.3 How to Achieve Compliance in the Cloud

To understand compliance in the Cloud, it is important to understand the concept of compliance inheritance. As mentioned before, many Cloud providers are certified for various regulations and industry requirements. Compliance inheritance means that the Cloud provider's infrastructure is out of scope for an organization's compliance audit, but everything the organization configures and builds on top of the certified services is still within scope. Compliance inheritance is shown in figure 6.5.

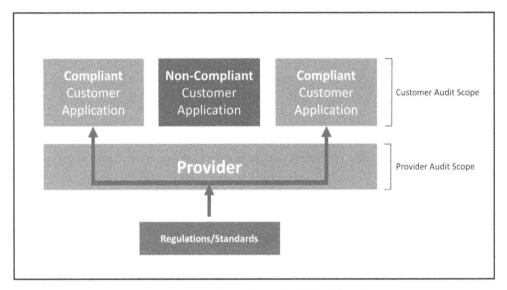

Figure 6.5 - Compliance In The Cloud

For example, if you should comply with PCI-DSS and during a Cloud provider evaluation process you find that the IaaS provider is PCI-DSS certified, then you are still ultimately responsible for building your own PCI-compliant service on that platform. The provider's infrastructure and operations should be outside the scope of your compliance, and you will fail your assessment to comply if you don't build your own services and applications properly.

Furthermore, it is important during the Cloud provider evaluation process to ask the provider where your data will be hosted, as many Cloud providers offer globally distributed data centers. It is your responsibility to manage and deploy data and services and still meet any legal compliance across national and international jurisdictions. Sometimes organizations place regulated data in a noncompliant country without even knowing that. Therefore, it is important to understand where your data is going to be located to stay compliant.

6.7　Security Threats in the Cloud

For many organizations, storing data in the Cloud might seem like a safe bet, and in most cases, it is. But risks always exist. Here are some serious security threats that you should be aware of when migrating your data to the Cloud.

6.7.1　Insecure Interfaces and APIs

Cloud providers expose sets of APIs (known as the management plane) that you use to manage and interact with Cloud services. Provisioning a VM through the Cloud management portal is an example of using such APIs. As with any piece of software, these APIs can contain software vulnerabilities, and to make it worse, these APIs are accessible via the internet, exposing them more broadly to potential exploitation.

Usually Cloud providers are responsible for most of the security of their management planes, but you should configure the right access management policies and assign roles (who can access the management plan and what they can do). A good practice is to require MFA when accessing the Cloud management plane and perhaps restricting which IPs can connect from the internet to these APIs.

6.7.2　Data Theft and Breaches

It is this kind of risk that is seen by every CIO as the worst nightmare, standing in front of the media and providing embarrassing assessments of the breach situation. This can even include potential lawsuits, like the recent famous incident with Equifax, where PII of over 143 million people was exposed.

While preventing data breaches is a shared responsibility between the Cloud provider and the customer, it is up to customers to come up with a plan to protect their data in the Cloud. This can be achieved in different ways, like encrypting sensitive information, applying proper access controls, using secure protocols, and monitoring audit logs.

6.7.3   Loss of Data

There is always a risk associated with data loss, but this risk has more threat agents when data is hosted in the Public Cloud. Of course, there is the threat of the attacker who steals or destroys data, but there is also the malicious insider who causes even worse damage.

But it does not need to be an attacker or a malicious insider who intentionally causes data loss. It can be a natural disaster, like a fire that takes down the whole data center. It can be an accidental mistake by the IT administrator who causes data loss by running a script that does some automation and accidently deletes a storage space. It can also be the loss of an encryption key, preventing access to encrypted data in the Cloud.

Sometimes organizations do not understand or poorly configure the native platform features offered by the Cloud provider, like assuming there are multiple copies of the data or that the backup job is running every day. For instance, small amounts of data were lost for some Amazon Web Services customers as its EC2 cloud suffered a remirroring storm due to human operator error on Easter weekend in 2011.

Although the chances of losing all your data in the Cloud are minimal, there have been incidents where attackers have gained access to Cloud data centers and wiped all the data clean. Therefore, it is important for organizations to distribute their applications across several zones and to back up data using off-site storage when possible. It is also worth asking the Cloud provider about their readiness to natural disasters and their availability/uptime percentages.

6.7.4   Denial of Service (DoS) and Distributed Denial-of-Service (DDoS)

Denial of Service (DoS) and distributed denial-of-service (DDoS) are both denial-of-service attacks. Such attacks flood servers, systems, and networks with traffic to overwhelm the victim's resources and make it difficult for legitimate users to access them.

DoS is when the attack is originating from one machine, while DDoS is when the attacker uses many machines (hundreds or thousands) to carry out the attack. Both attacks (DoS and DDoS) are surprisingly simple to implement, especially if the attacker has control of a botnet. Nowadays, attackers don't need to have the know-how or even own their own bots. All what they need is to transfer some of their cryptocurrency to buy the service from the dark web.

Usually attackers carry out a DoS or DDoS attack to gain the time they need to execute other types of attacks without getting caught. During such attacks, organizations can do nothing but sit and wait, and the Cloud provider will bill them for all resources consumed during the attack.

Many Cloud providers have systems in place to protect against DoS attacks, and they are offered free of charge. However, some Cloud providers offer more advanced protection services against such attacks as a paid service. For example, Amazon Shield is a managed DDoS protection service offered by Amazon and is available in a standard free tier and an advanced paid tier.

Moreover, organizations should be ready to scale when designing their applications hosted in the Cloud to meet additional traffic volumes, whether valid or from a DDoS attack, while having measures to identify what is normal volume and alerts on what is not.

A good practice also is to minimize the attack surface area by decoupling the infrastructure, such as separating the application from the database or the media from static content. This limits the internet access to critical components and moves the DDoS mitigation effort to only resources that are publicly accessible.

6.7.5   Malicious Insiders

This is considered a high impact threat that corresponds to the abuse of high privilege roles and can highly affect data confidentiality, integrity, and availability. To better study this threat in holistic manner, it should be analyzed from two distinct contexts:

- The insider is a malicious employee working for the Cloud provider.
- The insider is an employee of an organization using the Cloud.

The first case is the worst-case scenario for both the organization using the Cloud and for the Cloud provider. This can be, for example, an administrator working for the Cloud provider, who is responsible for performing regular backups for the data hosted in the Cloud and could exploit the fact that he can access sensitive information and do something bad with it (data leakage or destruction). It is the Cloud provider's responsibility to mitigate such risk by any means, although organizations can encrypt data at rest to protect the confidentiality of data stored in the Cloud.

The second case is also worth looking at. The insider is an employee of an organization that is using the Cloud and has administrative privileges on the Cloud's infrastructure and services. The insider knows the Cloud systems being used and can identify where sensitive data is located. Usually malicious insiders are motivated to steal valuable data, to get revenge, or to gain prestige.

While separation of duties can help mitigate such risk when it comes to the on-premises environment, it is hard to do so in a Cloud environment. This is because it is likely that the person who manages the Cloud infrastructure (like VMs) is the same person who configures firewall rules and the rest of services. Here are some countermeasures:

- Using anomaly detection to detect unusual behaviors.
- Using MFA.
- Using host-based instruction detection/prevention systems.
- Auditing logs.
- Implementing a Privileged Account Management system.

6.7.6   Reduce Visibility and Control

Using Cloud computing, that is, trusting the Cloud service provider to provide a set of services, operations, and assets depending on the service model in use, means that organizations lose some visibility and control over such assets and operations as the responsibility for some of the infrastructure moves to the Cloud provider.

Organizations using the Cloud should understand the shared responsibility model and distinguish between their responsibilities and the Cloud provider's. With reducing visibility and control, organizations must understand what services they are going to use, where their data will be hosted, and how to remain compliant after migrating to the Cloud.

6.7.7   Adjacent Vulnerability

One of the main characteristics of any Cloud is resource pooling, which means the Cloud provider abstracts resources and collects them into a pool of which can be allocated to different organizations. This is possible by using virtualization. Without virtualization, there is no Cloud.

However, this means that the same physical server can be processing data from different organizations (different tenants) at the same time. This might introduce a risk of an attacker or malicious user from one tenant, to expose or access resources from a different tenant, by exploiting a vulnerability in the virtualization stack (hypervisor). This risk covers failure of mechanisms separating storage, memory, routing, and even reputation among different tenants.

In the Cloud shared responsibility model, it is the Cloud provider's responsibility to secure the virtualization stack, enforce isolation, and maintain secure virtualization infrastructure. In this context, isolation ensures that computer processes or memory in one VM or container are not be visible to another. It is how Cloud providers separate different tenants, even if they are running processes on the same physical hardware.

6.7.8   Vendor Lock-In

When you move your data and workloads to one Cloud provider, it becomes difficult to migrate to another or migrate data and services back to an in-house IT environment. This makes organizations dependent on a Cloud provider for service provisioning, especially if data portability is not enabled. Organizations discover that the cost, effort, and time necessary for such a move is much higher than initially considered due to many factors like using proprietary tools from the Cloud provider or nonstandard APIs and data formats.

This risk increases in service models where the Cloud provider takes more responsibility, as in such models, the Cloud provider exposes more unique features, services, and APIs. Therefore, moving to a different Cloud provider requires changing these unique implementations. If an organization is only using VMs from one IaaS Cloud provider, it is much easier to move to another Cloud provider than if the organization is using a SaaS or PaaS services and features.

Of course, things can become bad if the Cloud provider goes out of business since the data can be lost or may not be able to be transferred to another Cloud provider in a timely manner. Therefore, it is important to learn the history and reputation of Cloud providers and read the SLA to see if there is a section addressing such a situation before moving data and workloads.

6.7.9   Insecure or Incomplete Data Deletion

Threats related to insecure or incomplete data deletion exist because organizations have reduced visibility into where the data is physically stored and a reduced ability to confirm the secure deletion of their data. The measures taken by an organization to delete data (e.g., destroying a disk) might not work in the Cloud, either because extra copies of data are stored but are not available or because the disk to be destroyed also stores data from other customers. Due to the multiple tenancies and reuse of hardware resources in the Cloud, this represents a higher risk to organizations than with dedicated hardware.

6.8   Other Topics

In this section, we cover more security topics that are worth looking at when migrating to the Cloud. There are some security capabilities that come with Cloud computing that are hard to implement on premises. Moreover, there are practices and concepts that become more important in the Cloud that you should carefully consider.

6.8.1 The Rise of Machine Learning in Cloud Security

Using Cloud computing opens the door for many opportunities that would be difficult to have on premises. Machine learning and AI are good examples. Not only is it expensive for organizations to invest in machine learning on premises, the visibility that Cloud providers have across their entire network gives them a clear advantage.

It is known that machine learning models consist of an algorithm and training data. The quality of the model depends on the data it's trained on. Cloud providers like Google, Amazon, and Azure have visibility across their entire network, which gives them a great opportunity to train their machine learning models on what is normal and what might be malicious.

There are many Cloud security services that use AI and machine learning to provide unique services that organizations can leverage. A good example is the *Identity Protection* service offered by Microsoft Azure Active Directory. This service analyzes authentication trends happening across the whole organization and detects anomalies and risky sign-ins. If John usually logs in during weekdays and never on weekends, then the service can raise a flag if it detects an authentication request from John during weekends and might even challenge John to perform an MFA first before allowing him to log in.

Amazon Macie is another good example of a machine-learning-powered service. This service recognizes sensitive data (such as PII or intellectual property) and provides visibility into where this data is stored and how it is being used. It can alert organizations to suspicious activity, such as the downloading of large amounts of content from unusual IP addresses or downloading sensitive information by a user who typically does not access this type of content. A compliance-focused capability of *Amazon Macie* detects if high-risk documents are shared publicly or to the entire company such as PII, PHI, IP, or legal data.

There are a lot of machine learning security tools available from many Cloud providers that are worth looking at. Such tools raise the bar for attackers and can help automate a lot of security tasks and management for organizations. The real benefit of machine-learning-based security tools is that they save organizations a lot of time and effort. Instead of having a human to look at a huge amount of data and security logs, machine learning automates all of that and points to what should be looked at.

6.8.2 Privileged Account Management

A recent report from Gartner reveals the top IT security projects for 2018 with privileged account management as a number-one priority project to initiate. Such projects can reduce the amount of risk and have the largest business impact. But why this is becoming more important with Cloud computing?

Organizations typically protected their internet access and internal resources like databases and web servers with top-of-the-line firewalls, IDS, IPS, and VPN access controls. This typical approach was used for almost thirty years, but with the huge adoption of the Cloud, this is no longer an effective solution alone. Do not forget that users are now using their mobile devices to access Cloud resources, which they can do from anywhere, and they use the public internet, which organizations do not have control over.

Therefore, privileged identities have become a new security perimeter, and organizations should have a proper privileged account management solution for accessing Cloud resources. Privileged access management is concerned with securing, monitoring, analyzing, and governing privileged access. It encourages the use of the *principle of least privilege*, where users are only assigned the minimum rights and privileges they need to carry on their tasks and nothing more.

If you are migrating to Microsoft Azure, then you can use *Microsoft Privileged Identity Management service (PIM)*. With PIM, users who are eligible for admin roles need to activate their admin roles before using them. During the activation process, they are required to perform an MFA to prove their identities. They also need to provide both a reason for activating and the duration for activation (e.g., two hours). After that time duration ends, their admin roles expire, and they are no longer active in their admin roles.

6.8.3 Just Enough Administration

It is not strange to see organizations assigning full admin rights to all users managing part of their Cloud infrastructure and resources. It is the easiest approach at first, as Cloud computing is a new playground, and no one wants something to break because of an access problem.

This also happens frequently when using migration tools or service accounts. If an organization is performing a SharePoint migration to the Cloud using a third-party tool, for example, then a full tenant-wide admin account is usually used as a service account to run the tool, instead of creating a more restricted service account with enough rights to run the tool.

If a script or an automation task should run in the Cloud, usually the account being used in this case is also a full global admin account that has full permissions and rights across the whole tenant.

Then there are contractors or consultants who are helping in the migration project and are given way more privileges in the Cloud environment than they ever need just because it is easier to use the full admin account.

However, many things can go wrong. A poorly written script that runs in the Cloud with high privileges can accidently damage the whole infrastructure, causing the deletion of resources or shutting down other Cloud services.

There are a lot of ways to mitigate such risk. First, organizations should understand the built-in admin roles defined in the Cloud platform they are using and possibly create more granular administrative roles to fit their needs.

Another important area of consideration is figuring out how to deploy Cloud resources with the *principle of least privilege* in mind. For example, an organization could deploy all workloads related to a specific project in a separate subscription and assign admin rights at the subscription level to specific teams working on the project.

6.8.4   What Is Changed in Logging?

Security logging and monitoring can be extremely tricky in a Cloud environment because of the rapid changes happening in the Cloud, where IP addresses are assigned dynamically in certain scenarios and the same IP address might be shared between two workloads over a short period of time (auto-scale set). Here are a couple of recommendations when considering security monitoring and logging:

- When inspecting log files, IP addresses might not be a good choice to identify a system or a workload, since the lifetime of an IP assignment is short in the Cloud. Also, some workloads like containers and serverless may not have a routable or recognizable IP at all. Instead, a more immutable identifier should be used.
- Due to the higher velocity of change, logs need to be offloaded and collected externally, as it is easy to lose logs in an auto-scale group if they are not collected before the instance shutdown.
- Customers should account for Cloud storage and networking cost when planning their monitoring and logging architecture. Customers might choose to send all logs to on-premises *Security Information and Event Management (SIEM)*.
- Host-level monitoring might not be available, especially for serverless deployment. In such case, the developer should write more robust application logging into the code.

6.8.5   Running Security Agents in the Cloud

It might be impossible to run a security control or agent (antivirus software) on a non-VM-based workload. How is it possible to run such agents on serverless workloads? Even if the workload is a VM, there are some recommendations when deploying agents in the Cloud.

- While traditional agents can be working just fine in your on-premises environment, they might badly affect performance in the Cloud. This is because it is common in the Cloud to have small VMs running very specific tasks compared to on-premises environment where it is common to have machines with high compute power running multiple services at once. Therefore, agents not designed for Cloud computing might increase processing overhead, requiring large and expensive VMs.

- Agents should take into consideration the elasticity of the Cloud and not rely on static IP address assignment to identify a system or communicate with the management system.

6.9   Conclusion

In this chapter, we talked about security and compliance in the Cloud and, most importantly, how Cloud computing forces organizations to think differently about both security and compliance. At the core of all this is the shared responsibility model. The Cloud provider is responsible for the security and compliance for parts of the Cloud stack that they manage, and the rest is your responsibility.

Compliance is different in the Cloud. By understanding the shared responsibility model, carefully evaluating Cloud providers, and asking the right questions, you can achieve compliance in the Cloud.

The Cloud opens the door for new security opportunities, also known as *security as a service.* Things like machine learning, AI, and anomaly detections are hard to implement on premises but are available to you *as a service* in the Cloud.

Is the Cloud secure? It depends on how you address security at each layer of the Cloud stack and learn the nature of the unique risks that come with Cloud computing. Only by carefully understanding how the Cloud operates and what you are responsible for securing, you can establish a security governance that can work for the Cloud.

About the Authors

José A. Hernández, a worldwide Cloud strategist advisor and migration expert with over 30 years of IT Consulting experience, and having the role of CTO for over 12 years, is a worldwide bestselling author of SAP books and a visionary of Cloud technology. Founded myCloudDoor in 2011, ever since helping enterprises adopting and migrating to Cloud Computing.

Ammar Hasayen, CISSP, Microsoft MVP is a leading expert on cybersecurity and cloud computing with over fifteen years of experience working with international enterprises. As a cloud security architect, Ammar helps organizations in their cloud migrations by adopting security best practices across the globe. He regularly writes and consults on variety of technical and security topics and runs blog.ahasayen.com. Ammar also speaks on many local and international conferences in the United States and Europe about cloud computing and cybersecurity, which makes him a well-known reference for both cloud and security best practices.

Javier Aguado. With a degree in Industrial Engineering specialized and Business Administration and Management, has worked as IT Consultant at NTT Data for several years, where he pushed Cloud technology and services. He joined myCloudDoor in 2016 as Cloud Service Director accompanying organizations in their Cloud Journey and has been performing Cloud Assessment and running Cloud Migration projects worldwide.

www.ingramcontent.com/pod-product-compliance
Lightning Source LLC
Chambersburg PA
CBHW051046050326
40690CB00006B/620